BOOK 2
PATTERNS
IN SPELLING
Patterns with Long Vowels

Teacher's Edition

TIM BROWN & DEBORAH F. KNIGHT

NEW READERS PRESS
Publishing Division of Laubach Literacy International
Syracuse, New York

About the Authors

Deborah Knight began her teaching career in the early 1970s and has taught both reading and English in urban, suburban, and rural settings. Since 1984, Ms. Knight has served as the Coordinator of the Learning Disabilities Assistance Program at Onondaga Community College in Syracuse, New York. Working closely with these OCC students, she has helped them to develop strategies for improving their reading, writing, spelling, and study skills.

Tim Brown has worked with developing and remedial readers and writers since 1978. He teaches courses in spelling as well as freshman composition and literature at Onondaga Community College. He also serves as Senior Professional Tutor at the college's Writing Skills Center, where he has a special interest in teaching spelling to developing and remedial writers and ESL students.

ON THE COVER: A quilt entitled *Rhythm/Color: Morris Men*, 99½" x 99½", by Michael James. This work of art appeared in *The Art Quilt* exhibit and book of the same name. It is reproduced here through the courtesy of The Quilt Digest Press.

ISBN 0-88336-103-5

© 1990

New Readers Press
Publishing Division of Laubach Literacy International
Box 131, Syracuse, New York 13210

Printed in the United States of America

Project Editor: Christina M. Jagger
Manuscript Editor: Mary Hutchison
Designed by Chris Steenwerth
Cover by Chris Steenwerth
Composition by Anne Hyde

9 8 7 6 5 4 3 2

Table of Contents

Glossary of Terms

affix A word element which carries meaning and is attached to a root word. Prefixes and suffixes are affixes; for example, *de-* and *-ful* in *delightful.*

blend The joining together of two or more sounds with each sound still being heard; for example, /tr/ in *trade.*

C A symbol representing any consonant.

compound word A word formed by combining two or more words. Compound words can be closed (*greenhouse*), hyphenated (*red-letter*), or open (*yellow jacket*).

diacritical mark A mark added to a letter to show how to pronounce the letter; for example, the straight line over a vowel to show a long vowel sound.

digraph A pair of letters which represent one sound; for example, *ch* making the sound /ch/ in *chain* and *ea* making the sound /ē/ in *sea.*

family A letter pattern or sequence such as *ine* in *fine, mine,* and *combine.* The pattern usually forms a common syllable ending and is composed of a vowel or vowel combination plus the consonant(s) that go with it.

homonym One of a pair or more of words having the same sound but different meanings and often different spellings; for example, *tail* and *tale.*

pattern A recurrent, usually predictable sequence of letters. Patterns occur in common syllables (e.g., *ope*) as well as in prefixes, suffixes, roots, and compound words. Spelling rules also produce patterns.

prefix A word element which carries meaning and is attached to the beginning of a root word; for example, *pre-* in *prepaid.*

schwa A vowel sound that usually occurs in unstressed syllables in English as heard in the first syllable of *against*; also the symbol (ə) often used to represent the sound.

sight word A word which is not phonetically predictable; also any word for which students have not had the phonics to enable them to spell the word phonetically.

suffix A word element which carries meaning and is attached to the end of a root word; for example, *-less* in *speechless.*

syllable A spoken unit of uninterrupted sound containing one vowel sound producing either a word (e.g., *pay*) or a distinct part of a word (e.g., *pay* or *ment* in *payment*); the letters producing that sound in the word.

V A symbol representing any vowel.

Style Notes

/x/ A letter between slashes indicates a sound rather than a spelling; for instance /b/ is the sound produced by the letter *b.*

/ĭ/ A curved mark (breve) over a vowel indicates the short vowel sound.

/ī/ A straight line (macron) over a vowel indicates the long vowel sound.

/ə/ This indicates the schwa sound.

S: This indicates something said by the student.

T: This indicates something said by the teacher or tutor.

1. Overview of the Series

Patterns in Spelling provides students with a powerful, systematic method of learning to spell by stressing the patterns that are regularly found in English words. Many patterns included in this series are word families composed of syllables or syllable endings—for example, *ot, ight, ed,* and *ouse.* Other patterns are based on consonant blends and digraphs. This approach emphasizes the regularities of spelling more strongly than does a purely phonics-based approach. It is highly effective with adults who are just learning to read and write as well as with adults and older teens who may know how to read but who have failed to learn to spell using a more traditional, straight-phonics approach.

The Pattern Approach

In the pattern approach, students learn to perceive that words contain a common pattern plus other letters. This method simplifies the task of learning to spell. Rather than studying sequences of individual letters, students study the spelling of the pattern as a unit. At the same time, students learn the pronunciation of the pattern. For instance, in Lesson 18 of Book 2, students study the *ight* pattern, learning that the spelling unit *i-g-h-t* makes the sound unit /īt/ and that /īt/ is spelled *i-g-h-t*. Then they study several representative words containing the pattern. Instead of having to learn the sequence of five letters to spell *light,* they learn a two-part sequence: *l* plus the *ight* pattern.

The pattern approach simplifies learning to spell the representative words presented in the lessons. It also provides students with an effective tool to predict the spelling of other words containing a particular sound unit. For instance, in Lesson 6 of Book 1, students study the *ill* pattern, learning that *ill* makes the sound /ĭl/ and that /ĭl/ is spelled *i-l-l*. They also study four representative words. But once students know that /ĭl/ is spelled *i-l-l* at the end of words, they should be able to spell other words belonging to this family. To reinforce this concept, they are asked to write many words ending with the *ill* pattern later in the lesson.

The Discovery Approach

Throughout the series students are given exercises designed to help them discover patterns and rules. For instance, this method is used when students are learning about doubling a final consonant or dropping the final *e* before adding an ending beginning with a vowel. This inductive approach is in direct contrast to the usual approach of giving students a rule first and having them memorize it and then apply it. We believe that students are more likely to remember the pattern because they have figured it out for themselves.

Three Modes of Learning to Spell

This series integrates three ways of learning to spell—hearing, seeing, and writing the words. As students use these three modes to learn the spelling of a word, they are simultaneously developing three memories for the word—their memory for the way the word sounds, their memory for the way the word looks, and their memory for how it feels to write the word. By using three modes instead of only one, they learn the word more thoroughly. And when they need to spell the word, they have three ways to access its correct spelling.

Spelling as a Means to an End

When students are learning to spell, it is helpful to concentrate on words in isolation. Thus a number of exercises in this series deal only with the correct spelling of words. But in real life, spelling is generally only one element of a more complex writing task. So this series also includes various types of writing activities that students encounter in school, at home, and on the job. These activities are designed to help students transfer the spelling skills they are learning to real-life situations.

The Components of the Series

This series contains four student books, four teacher's editions of the student books, and a diagnostic/placement test. Each of the four books emphasizes one aspect of spelling: short vowels, long vowels, consonant blends and digraphs, and other vowel sounds.

Book 1: Patterns with Short Vowels presents word families containing short vowels. Common syllable consonant endings are grouped with the short vowel sounds to produce the word families. The vowels are presented in the order: *i, u, e, o, a*. The non-alphabetic order separates short vowel sounds that sound similar, particularly short *e* and *i*, to make it easier for students to learn and discriminate between them.

Book 2: Patterns with Long Vowels presents word families containing the long vowels: *a, e, i,* and *o*. Long *u*, with its two sounds, is presented in Book 4. The most common patterns for spelling long vowel sounds are presented, along with strategies for learning homonyms and correct spellings when more than one would be phonetically correct.

Book 3: Patterns with Consonant Blends and Digraphs presents beginning and ending consonant blends, digraphs that can be positioned at either the beginning or end of syllables, and silent consonants.

Book 4: Patterns with Other Vowel Sounds and Spellings presents word families containing vowel sounds that are more difficult to spell. These include less common spellings of long and short vowel sounds, r-controlled vowels, and other vowel sounds such as /oi/.

The teacher's editions provide teaching suggestions, unit tests, and reduced replicas of the student pages with answers filled in.

The diagnostic/placement test is designed to determine which prerequisite spelling skills students possess and which they lack, and to help you place students in the proper book in the series. The test can be administered to either an individual or a group. Specific descriptions of the subtests and their use and interpretation are found in the teacher's edition of the diagnostic test.

2. Introduction to Book 2

Book 2 of *Patterns in Spelling* presents the most common patterns for spelling the long vowels *a, e, i,* and *o.* In addition, Book 2 stresses several spelling strategies and skills: choosing the correct spelling of phonetically correct alternatives or homonym pairs, recognizing common syllable types, writing words of two or more syllables, finding root words, recognizing irregular forms of verbs, and using guide words to find words in the dictionary. Several patterns for adding endings are also covered, including dropping a final silent *e* when adding an ending that starts with a vowel, and adding endings to words that end in a consonant plus *y, f* or *fe, o,* and *oe.* Patterns learned in Book 1 are also reviewed.

Starting Students in Book 2

To begin this series in Book 2, students need to have in place certain prerequisite skills: knowing the basic sound/symbol relationships, and being able to write the alphabet in sequence, to hear letter sounds and syllables, and to rhyme. They also need to be able to spell simple words containing short vowel sounds—the theme of Book 1. These skills are tested in the diagnostic/placement inventory. Be sure that students achieve satisfactory scores on the prerequisite skills subtests and mastery on the short vowel subtest before you consider starting them in Book 2.

To start this series in Book 2, students should also be familiar with the other important spelling material introduced in Book 1. This material includes the pattern for doubling the final consonant of **CVC** words when adding endings that begin with a vowel; adding *-s* and *-es* to nouns and verbs; forming the singular possessive, contractions, and compound words; identifying root words; dividing words into syllables; and hyphenating numbers. Many exercises in Book 1 also develop skills for using the dictionary, such as alphabetizing words by the third, fourth, and fifth letters; finding words in the dictionary; using guide words; recognizing the schwa and short vowel symbols; and using the pronunciation guide. These are all skills that students need in order to be successful in Book 2.

Consonant Blends and Digraphs in Book 2

A number of the representative family words in Book 2 contain consonant blends and digraphs. Some of these words are common words that students need to know how to spell. Others are included to make students aware that there are many words in the English language that contain these families. If your students have trouble learning to spell some of the words containing consonant blends and digraphs, have them concentrate on learning the common words that they use regularly. Do not be too concerned if they have trouble learning to spell the more difficult words. Strategies for learning consonant blends and digraphs are dealt with in detail in Book 3 of this series.

The Glossary and Style Notes

A glossary of terms and an explanation of the symbols used in this book are found on page four of this book. They are also included on the last page of the student text. As you are introducing students to Book 2, draw their attention to this reference material and discuss the terms as they encounter them in their lessons.

3. How to Use the Series

Patterns in Spelling is designed to make students aware that the spelling of the English language is actually quite regular, although complex. For this series to be successful in teaching students how to spell, you need to accept this premise and emphasize the regularity of the language.

The four workbooks in this series are designed to be used sequentially. Administer the diagnostic/placement test to determine which book each student should start in.

Students should not try to learn the spelling of phonetic patterns before they can sight-read words containing those patterns. If your students are learning to read as well as learning to spell, be sure they have been introduced to the necessary phonics in their reading. The order in which the word families are introduced in *Patterns in Spelling* basically corresponds to the sequence found in the *Laubach Way to Reading, Focus on Phonics,* and the *Challenger Adult Reading Series*.

The American Heritage Dictionary is used as the primary reference dictionary for this series. Since dictionaries are not uniform in their use of diacritical marks, some translation of our dictionary exercises may be necessary if your students are using another dictionary.

The Recommended Lesson Format

Before beginning to teach a lesson, you should carefully examine the word families, representative words, and lesson notes. In addition, you should develop any additional practice exercises you anticipate might be necessary.

Exactly how you decide to use these lessons will be determined by the number of students you have, the level of your students, the number of times you meet with students each week, and other variables. The following format is suggested for use with a group of students who are all working on the same lesson. In general, it is recommended that each lesson be taught over three class periods. Here is an overview of the suggested three-day format.

Day 1

1. Give a pretest on the sight words and then go over the sight words.
2. Present the listening exercise which deals with the word family words.
3. Complete all exercises related to the word family words and sight words except for the writing sentences exercise.
4. Assign studying the sight words and word family words as homework.

Day 2

1. Review the sight words and give a practice quiz on them.
2. Do the listening exercise again.
3. Introduce the other material presented in the lesson and complete the corresponding exercises either in class or for homework.
4. Assign as homework preparing for spelling quizzes on both the sight words and the word family words.

Day 3

1. Do the listening exercise once more.
2. Review new material introduced in the lesson and go over any exercises done for homework.
3. Complete the writing sentences exercise.
4. Give two graded spelling quizzes for the lesson—one on the sight words and the other on selected words belonging to the word families introduced in the lesson.

Day 1 in Detail

1. Introduce the Sight Words

Many lessons in the series contain sight words—words which are not phonetically predictable or words for which the phonics necessary to spell them have not yet been introduced. Some words which appear as sight words early in the series will become predictable when the word families to which these sight words belong are introduced.

Remember that the two major steps to achieving the correct spelling of a sight word are: 1. remembering that the spelling of the word is not predictable in most cases and 2. recalling and producing the correct spelling.

Begin each lesson with a pretest of the sight words. Give the pretest before students have looked at the sight word list. Instruct students to leave three blank lines between each word. To give the pretest:

1. Say each sight word.
2. Use it in a simple sentence.
3. Say the sight word again.

Next have students open their books to the lesson and correct the pretest.

1. For each misspelled word, have the students underline any parts spelled correctly. This will help students to realize how much of each word they already know how to spell.

2. For each sight word, have the students write the correct spelling three times in a column to the right, even if the spelling in the pretest was correct. Students should say the word as they write it. In a classroom setting this can be conducted as a group activity.

3. When appropriate, help students to develop memory devices for difficult words. Do this by having students relate the sight words to words they already know how to spell. For example, *weight* becomes relatively easy to learn if the end spelling is associated with *eight*, an early sight word; *only* won't be misspelled *ownly* if its meaning and spelling are associated with the related word *one*. Make sure students write the memory devices near the list of sight words in their books. Do not have students generate memory devices for words that do not give them trouble.

Do not spend too much time on the sight words. The next activity, the listening exercise, is the most important part of the lesson.

2. Present the Listening Exercise

The listening exercise, Exercise 1 in each lesson, is core to this series. It teaches students to develop a systematic approach to analyzing words.

The listening exercise uses a variety of modes—seeing the words, hearing the words, and spelling the words—to help students to learn them. As students examine each word family, they follow a four-step process:

Step 1: They listen to the pronunciation of the word family and then they spell the family.

Step 2: They listen to the spelling of the word family and then they give the pronunciation of the family.

Step 3: They listen to each word in the word family, one at a time. They spell the word family and then the other sound(s) in the word.

Step 4: They listen to the word and then they spell the whole word.

A model of how to present the listening exercise is given in Lesson 1. Study this model and faithfully follow it. In general, we believe that you know your students best and should adapt materials to meet their needs and your teaching style. In the case of the listening exercise, however, you must adhere to the procedure if this approach is to be effective.

Notice that the words in each column are arranged so that the word family in all the words line up. This was done to help train students to see the word family in each word. You should point this out to your students.

As you are going over the words in the word family lists, concentrate on the shorter words in the family. The longer words are included to show students that the word families they are learning will help them to spell more complex words and to give them practice in recognizing the sounds in words of two or more syllables. Be sure that your students understand that the word family lists contain representative words and that usually there are many more words that belong to each family.

3. Do Exercises Related to Word Family Words and Sight Words

Have students complete the one or two exercises related to the word family words and sight words which follow the listening exercise. The lesson notes explain how to do these exercises. In some exercises, you will have to dictate words to students. They can complete other exercises by themselves or in small groups.

As students are working on the exercises, observe what they are doing. If you see a student making errors in an exercise, correct the student quickly before he has a chance to reinforce a misconception.

4. Assign Homework

Have students study the sight words and the word family words for homework. Teach students to use the four-step methods outlined on the next page.

As you are introducing these methods, point out the similarities and differences between the steps for studying sight words and those for studying word family words. Help students to practice the methods during class until they have learned them. You may photocopy these instructions and give them to students.

How to Study Sight Words

1. **Say the word.**
   - Listen for the consonant and vowel sounds.

2. **Look at the word.**
   - Study the sequence of letters. Note the letters that spell the sounds.
   - Pay special attention to the part of the word you misspelled on the pretest. If you have a memory device for that word, study it.

3. **Think about the word.**
   - Think about how it sounds.
   - Think about how it looks.
   - Think about the memory device, if you have one.

4. **Write the word.**
   - Ask yourself, "Does the word look right?"
   - Check the spelling of the word.
   - Write the word again if you are not sure of the spelling.

How to Study Word Family Words

1. **Say the word.**
   - Train yourself to listen for the word family plus the other sounds.

2. **Look at the word.**
   - Study the sequence of letters. Note the letters that spell the sounds.
   - Train yourself to see the word as the word family plus the other letters.

3. **Think about the word.**
   - Think about how it sounds.
   - Think about how it looks.
   - Think about the word as the word family plus the other letters.

4. **Write the word.**
   - Ask yourself, "Does the word look right?"
   - Check the spelling of the word.
   - Write the word again if you are not sure of the spelling.

Day 2 in Detail

1. Review the Sight Words

Give an ungraded practice quiz on all the sight words in the lesson. Use the same procedure as you did for the pretest—saying the word, using it in a sentence, and saying it again. Students do not need to skip three lines between words this time.

Have students correct the quiz by checking their spelling against the sight word list. You should take a quick look at their quizzes, since poor spellers often do not catch all their misspelled words.

If students need additional help learning the sight words, give them a drill exercise such as one of the following:

- Have students copy the words they misspelled.
- Have them copy short phrases or sentences which include words they misspelled. You will need to make these up ahead of time.
- Have them make up and write short phrases or sentences containing the words they missed.

2. Review the Listening Exercise

Go over the listening exercise again. Continue to emphasize the word family in each word in the word lists. Although this may seem tedious, it is essential in order to develop in students a sense of the structure and pattern of language, which then permits them to systematically analyze the spelling of words.

3. Introduce the Other Material Presented in the Lesson

Each lesson also includes work in such areas as adding endings, dictionary work, homonyms, and writing activities. Introduce this material and have students complete the corresponding exercises either in class or for homework. The lesson notes explain how to present these exercises.

4. Assign Homework

Have students prepare for graded quizzes on the sight words and the word family words. Also have students review any new material you introduced today. They should complete exercises related to the new material if they did not do those exercises during class.

Day 3 in Detail

1. Review the Listening Exercise

Go over the listening exercise again. Continue to emphasize the word family in each word in the word lists.

2. Review the Other Material Presented in the Lesson

Review any other material presented in the lesson and go over any exercises done for homework. If students have had trouble with the material either in the exercises or the dictation sentences, you may need to develop additional exercises to reinforce it.

3. Complete the Writing Sentences Exercise

You will need to dictate the sentences in this exercise. These sentences include sight words, word family words, and other material from the current lesson.

You may need to dictate the longer sentences twice. Encourage students to listen to the entire sentence and repeat it to themselves before they begin to write. This strategy will help students to develop their skill in remembering what they hear—an important skill for success in both academic and everyday situations.

After students have written the sentences, have them pair up and compare their sentences. At the same time, you should also quickly check their sentences. Pay particular attention to the spelling of the sight words and word family words and their ability to apply the other material presented in the lesson.

4. Give Spelling Quizzes

Give two graded spelling quizzes. One quiz should contain all the sight words. The other quiz should consist of representative words from the word families introduced in the lesson. In general, we recommend that you select 10 to 15 words for this quiz. Use your own judgment about which words to select. If your students are having trouble with spelling, you may want to include only one-syllable words and avoid the more difficult blends and digraphs. If your students are doing quite well, you might include the words of two or more syllables, or you might include words which belong to the word families but which were not listed in the listening exercise. Use the usual procedure for dictating words.

You should correct these quizzes. Students should have mastered these words by this time and should not misspell more than one word on each quiz.

Have students keep two separate personal spelling lists in their notebooks. One list should contain sight words they misspelled on their quizzes. The other list should contain misspelled word family words. When students misspell a word on a quiz, have them add the word to the appropriate list. Have students copy their lists once a day, saying each word as they write it.

Give students the opportunity to take spelling quizzes on their personal spelling lists periodically. They can check off words on their lists when they have mastered them. This will give them a sense of accomplishment.

How to Use the Unit and Book Reviews

Reviews for each unit and for each book provide additional reviews of sight words, word families, and skills that have been presented and reinforced in the lessons. Suggested words for unit and book spelling tests are included in the notes for each review.

We suggest that you use two class sessions to complete each review. Divide the work into manageable units. You will probably want students to complete some exercises in class with your assistance. You may decide to preview other exercises in class and have students complete them as part of their homework. Also as part of their homework, students should review the sight words and representative word family words in preparation for the unit spelling tests. They should pay particular attention to words on their personal spelling lists.

Suggested word lists for both word family and sight words are included in the notes for each review. However, you may want to adapt these tests to emphasize words your students are having particular trouble with. Correctly spelling 90 percent of the words on each test should be considered mastery. Have students cross out any words on their personal spelling lists which they have now mastered. Also have them add any misspelled words to the appropriate list.

Adapting the Lesson Format

This series can be successfully used in tutorial, small group, and large group settings. The recommended lesson format was designed to be used with a small group of students who are all working on the same lesson. If you are tutoring a single student, or if your students are working on different levels, you may want to revise the recommended format to meet the needs of your special situation. The suggestions which follow are intended to help you make the best use of this series.

Tutoring a Single Student

The word families approach to spelling has been used successfully in a tutorial setting using the recommended lesson format. You may be able to cover the material a bit faster when working with a single student. You certainly will be able to observe a single student closely and gear the pace of the material to meet that student's needs. Avoid the temptation of helping the student so much that he or she does not have the opportunity to take full advantage of the discovery approach.

Teaching Students at Different Levels

It is possible that, based on the results of the diagnostic/placement test, students may be working in any of the four books and you may have as many as four groups to deal with. Here are some suggestions for working out ways to spend time with each group.

- Have different groups working on different parts of the lessons on any given day. For example, the Book 1 group might be working on the Day 1 material, the Book 2 group might be working on the Day 2 material, and so on. At least one group may not work on spelling at all on a given day.

- Spend the beginning of class with one group. Spend the latter part of class with another group. The groups that you are not working with directly can be working on other material.

- Audiotape the sight words pretests and practice tests, the dictation exercises, and the two spelling quizzes. This will prove to be a great timesaver for you—especially if you are dealing with several groups or if absenteeism is a problem.

- Have a reliable student who is working in one of the later spelling books give some of the quizzes and tests to students working in earlier books.

4. Other Considerations

Building Spelling Awareness

As students work through *Patterns in Spelling*, they should develop a sense of their personal spelling strengths and weaknesses. This sense should come not only from the words they are exposed to in the series but also from the words they use in their writing. Beginning spellers tend to feel that they are weak in all areas, and, indeed, it may require some time for relative strengths and weaknesses to show themselves. But it will become evident, for instance, that a student has more trouble with some vowel sounds than others.

Look for recurring patterns of strength and weakness in students' spelling. Examine their personal spelling lists and their writing. Does one student spell phonetically and thus correctly spell words that follow phonic principles but misspell those that do not? Does another student have more trouble spelling the middle of words than the beginning or end? Do errors involve specific short vowel sounds or consonant digraphs?

Help students to develop a sense of their spelling strengths. If they regularly spell word family words correctly or accurately apply the pattern for doubling the final consonant, point this out to them. You can also point out how many words they are learning to spell by having them examine the word family and sight word lists which appear at the back of each book. Also point out the many words that they are spelling correctly in their writing. As students become aware of personal spelling strengths, they begin to feel confident about their spelling and are better able to focus their learning attention on areas of weakness.

Help students to detect those areas of weakness. Students who are aware of their weaknesses can address them more directly than students who are not. Once a student is aware of a weakness, two things should be done. The student should begin to give the area of weakness extra attention and study and be encouraged to develop a healthy sense of doubt when writing words that fall into the area of weakness. If, for example, a student has difficulty applying the doubling of the final consonant pattern, lessons that deal with this should be reviewed for homework. In written work, the student should be encouraged to proofread for words that are built from roots ending with a consonant-vowel-consonant pattern. He should then check his spelling of the word against what is predicted by the pattern before checking the spelling in a dictionary.

Misspelled Words in Students' Writing

Errors in students' writing can be divided into two broad categories: those in words that students have studied and those in words that students have not yet studied. Each group can be informative.

Try to determine the source of the errors in words that have been studied. Does the evidence suggest that the student has misunderstood something, has failed to make a connection between spelling and meaning, has not studied enough, or has a poor visual memory for words he has studied?

Misspelled words that have not been studied can be handled in a variety of ways. If a student has misspelled many words in a piece of writing, pointing out all of them can discourage the student. We suggest that you again look for patterns. If you find a pattern and address it, you will be teaching the student to spell a number of words correctly rather than just one.

You might also consider pointing out high utility words—ones students are apt to use frequently. Learning to spell such words correctly will considerably cut down on the number of words misspelled.

Also consider asking students which misspelled words they most want to learn to spell. Adult learners, particularly, should have some control over what they learn.

Have your students create a third personal word list for words they misspell in their writing. You might suggest that they buy a small notebook and devote one page to each letter of the alphabet. As students enter words that are troublesome to them, they create their own personal dictionaries. They can carry these with them and easily refer to them.

Errors in words that have not been studied should not be treated negatively. Find something to praise, even if it is only the effort. Take the time to point out what was done correctly. Remember that your students may be attempting things beyond their skill level.

A Last Word

To a certain degree, success in spelling correlates to students' understanding and appreciation of the language as a whole. This series attempts to instill in students an understanding, appreciation, and enjoyment of language. But no series can hope to be responsive to all the questions students have. You can greatly enhance the learning experience by encouraging questions about the language and correlating what the student is learning in spelling to what the student is learning in reading or other areas of study.

Scope and Sequence: Book 2

Word Families — Lesson	1	2	3	4	5	6	R1	7	8	9	10	11	12	13	14	R2	15	16	17	18	R3	19	20	21	22	23	R4	BR
Learn words containing long vowel word families:																												
1. Long *a* families	●	●	●	●	●	●																						●
2. Long *e* families		●	●	●	●			●	●																			●
3. Long *i* families				●	●			●	●								●	●	●	●		●						●
4. Long *o* families					●	●			●	●										●	●	●	●	●			●	●

Word Study — Lesson	1	2	3	4	5	6	R1	7	8	9	10	11	12	13	14	R2	15	16	17	18	R3	19	20	21	22	23	R4	BR
1. Spell sight words	●	●	●	●	●	●	●	●	●	●	●	●	●	●	●	●	●	●	●	●	●	●	●	●	●	●	●	●
Months of the year	●	●																										
Direction words			●																									
Measurement words																			●					●				
2. Learn/review spelling patterns:																												
Silent *e* Pattern 1	●	●	●			●	●						●			●	●	●				●						●
Patterns that spell long *a*: aCe, aiC, aCCe, *ay*, aCy	●	●	●	●		●	●						●			●	●					●						●
Patterns that spell long *e*: *e, ee, ea, ey, y*, eCe											●	●			●													●
Double consonants in the middle of words												●	●															
Changing *y* to *i*														●	●			●	●									●
Forming the plural of words that end in C*y*														●	●			●	●									●
Patterns that spell long *i*: iCe, *y, igh, ign*, iCd																	●			●								●
Changing *f* to *v*																		●										
Doubling Pattern 1																					●							●
The ending *-es*																					●							●
Patterns that spell long *o*: oCe, olC, oaC, *o, oe, ow, own*										●						●		●		●								●
Adding endings to words that end in *o* and *oe*																						●	●					●
3. Learn principal parts of verbs with long vowel sounds		●														●		●		●			●					
4. Learn how to write dates		●																										
5. Capitalize direction words			●																									
6. Learn alternative spellings for the same sound:																												
/ās/ spelled *ace* or *ase*			●	●																								●
aCe or aiC				●	●																							
/īz/ spelled *ise* or *ize*																			●	●								●
/ōz/ spelled *ose* or *oze*																						●						
/ōl/ spelled *ole* or *oll*																							●	●			●	
/ōld/ spelled *old, oled,* or *olled*																							●	●	●		●	●
7. Spell homonyms				●	●	●	●				●	●	●		●										●	●		●
8. Learn mnemonic devices	●			●																								

Word Study

Lesson	1	2	3	4	5	6	R1	7	8	9	10	11	12	13	14	R2	15	16	17	18	R3	19	20	21	22	23	R4	BR
9. Discriminate between similar sounds																				●					●			●
10. Identify the number of syllables in words						●																						
11. Review the days of the week and their abbreviations						●																						
12. Complete crossword puzzles							●									●				●							●	

Word Structure

Lesson	1	2	3	4	5	6	R1	7	8	9	10	11	12	13	14	R2	15	16	17	18	R3	19	20	21	22	23	R4	BR
1. Add endings:																												
to words that end in silent *e*	●		●				●						●			●	●	●	●	●		●	●					●
-ed and *-ing* to verbs	●		●													●	●	●	●	●		●	●					●
to words that end in C*y*														●					●	●			●					●
-es to words that end in *f* or *fe*																		●		●		●		●				●
to **CVC** words																●				●		●						●
to words that end in *oe*																										●		●
-s or *-es* to words that end in *o*																										●		●
2. Identify root words	●		●				●										●				●							●
3. Add affixes to root words			●				●							●	●	●			●	●		●	●					●
4. Build words using initial consonants and word families				●		●	●		●	●	●	●				●	●	●		●	●	●		●	●			●
5. Write words by syllables						●	●		●	●	●	●	●	●	●	●			●	●	●	●		●	●			●
6. Recognize/identify/categorize syllable types:																												
Closed (**CVC**)								●	●	●	●	●	●	●	●	●	●	●			●	●		●				●
Cle								●	●	●		●	●	●		●	●	●			●	●						●
VCe								●	●	●	●	●	●	●	●	●	●	●		●	●	●	●	●	●			●
Open								●	●	●	●	●	●		●	●	●	●		●	●	●	●	●				●
Double vowel									●	●	●	●	●		●	●	●	●		●	●	●	●	●				●
7. Study suffixes:																												
-teen										●					●													
-ly														●	●	●												
8. Combine syllables to form words																●	●									●		●
9. Spell unfamiliar names																	●											

Writing

Lesson	1	2	3	4	5	6	R1	7	8	9	10	11	12	13	14	R2	15	16	17	18	R3	19	20	21	22	23	R4	BR
1. Write words from dictation	●	●	●	●	●	●	●	●	●	●	●	●	●	●	●	●	●	●	●	●	●	●	●	●	●	●	●	●
2. Write sentences from dictation	●	●	●		●	●	●	●	●	●	●	●	●	●	●	●	●	●	●	●	●	●	●	●	●	●	●	●
3. Complete cloze exercises	●																						●					
4. Complete sentences	●	●	●		●		●			●			●			●		●		●	●			●		●	●	
5. Compose sentences		●	●		●	●	●			●		●				●	●		●				●		●	●		
6. Compose paragraphs				●			●								●									●				●

Writing	Lesson	1	2	3	4	5	6	R1	7	8	9	10	11	12	13	14	R2	15	16	17	18	R3	19	20	21	22	23	R4	BR
7. Fill out Forms								●																					
Dictionary Skills	**Lesson**	1	2	3	4	5	6	R1	7	8	9	10	11	12	13	14	R2	15	16	17	18	R3	19	20	21	22	23	R4	BR
1. Alphabetize words		●	●																										
2. Learn the long vowel symbol			●			●								●							●				●				
3. Find abbreviations				●																●						●			
4. Find irregular verb forms			●				●				●					●	●						●		●		●		
5. Determine homonym spellings					●		●					●			●		●								●	●			
6. Select from alternative spellings						●										●					●								
7. Learn the meaning of words						●					●				●	●	●									●			
8. Use guide words												●				●													
9. Find names in a directory																	●												
10. Find the plural of words that end in *o*																										●		●

Lesson 1
The Word Families *ake, ame, ade, ate*, and *ape*
Objectives

- **Word Families:** Learn to spell words in the *ake, ame, ade, ate,* and *ape* families.
- **Sight Words:** Learn to spell *January, February, March, April, May,* and *June.* Learn a saying for remembering the number of days in each month.
- **Dictionary Skills:** Review alphabetizing words by the first two or three letters.
- **Patterns:** Discover that a silent *e* at the end of a word usually produces a long vowel sound. Discover Silent *e* Pattern 1.
- **Endings:** Practice dropping the final silent *e* when adding *-ed* and *-ing* to verbs.
- **Using Words in Context:** Complete a paragraph by filling in word family words.
- **Writing Sentences:** Practice writing word family and sight words in context.

Sight Words

Teach the sight words using the methods described on pages 9-12 in the introduction to this book. Make special note of the first *r* in *February*. Many students will misspell *February* because they don't pronounce this *r*.

❶ Listening

Introduce the words in the *ake* family using the following method.

T: Look at the first group of words. These words belong to the *ake* family. Listen to the sound /āk/. (Say *ake*.) What letters make the sound /āk/?
S: *A-k-e.*
T: Good. Do you hear the letter *e*?
S: No.
T: Right. The letter *e* is silent, but it does make the *a* sound long. (Say /ā/.) Now, what sound do the letters *a-k-e* make?

Lesson 1
The Word Families *ake, ame, ade, ate*, and *ape*

Sight Words		
January	March	May
February	April	June

Word Families

❶ Listening

ake

Listen to the sound *ake* makes in these words.

cake	take	wake	shake
bake	stake	awake	brake
baker	mistake	snake	brake fluid

ame

Listen to the sound *ame* makes in these words.

name	came	blame	frame
same	became	flame	framed

ade

Listen to the sound *ade* makes in these words.

made	shade	grade	parade
wade	spade	trade	lemonade

ate

Listen to the sound *ate* makes in these words.

ate	late	plate	fascinate
fate	later	state	exaggerate
gate	lately	locate	United States

ape

Listen to the sound *ape* makes in these words.

cape	drape	tape	scrape
escape	grape	shape	scraper

4　　Lesson 1

S: /āk/.
T: Good. Listen to the /āk/ sound in the word *cake*. (Say *cake*.) Now listen again. (Say *cake* again.) What letters make the sound /āk/?
S: *A-k-e.*
T: Good. What letter makes the first /k/ sound in *cake*?
S: *C.*
T: Good. What letters spell *cake*?
S: *C-a-k-e.*
T: Now look at the second word. Listen to the /āk/ sound in the word *bake*. (Say *bake*.) What letters make the sound /āk/?
S: *A-k-e.*

T: Good. What letter makes the /b/ sound in *bake*?
S: *B.*
T: Good. What letters spell *bake*?
S: *B-a-k-e.*
T: What does *c-a-k-e* spell?
S: *Cake.*
T: What does *b-a-k-e* spell?
S: *Bake.*

Emphasize that by changing the beginning of a word, you can make new words.

T: What is the difference in the spellings of *cake* and *bake*?
S: *Cake* starts with a *c* and *bake* starts with a *b*.

❷ Writing Words. On the lines below, write the words that you hear.

1. _made_   4. _name_   7. _baker_
2. _later_   5. _grade_   8. _locate_
3. _make_   6. _cape_   9. _became_

❸ Dictionary Skills: Alphabetizing. On the lines below, alphabetize the words in Exercise 2.

1. _baker_   4. _grade_   7. _made_
2. _became_   5. _later_   8. _make_
3. _cape_   6. _locate_   9. _name_

❹ Using Sight Words. Fill in the missing months in this well-known saying.

Thirty days have September, ___April___, ___June___, and November. All the rest have 31 except ___February___, which has 28.

❺ Finding a Pattern. The long vowel sounds are the same as the names of the vowels. For example, the long *a* sound is the same as the letter *a*. Listen to the sound the *a* makes in the pairs of words below. In each pair, underline the word that has the long *a* sound. Then put a long vowel mark (⁻) over the long *a* in each word you underlined.

1. at   āte   4. Sam   sāme   7. fāte   fat
2. mad   māde   5. rāte   rat   8. tap   tāpe
3. hāte   hat   6. cap   cāpe   9. glāde   glad

What is the final letter in all the words that have the long *a* sound? ___e___

Can you hear the final letter in the long *a* words? ___no___

Pattern: Words with a long vowel sound often end with a silent *e*.

Lesson 1   5

T: Good. What is the difference in meaning between *cake* and *bake*?
S: *Cake* means "a dessert food" and *bake* means "to cook in an oven."
T: Good. Notice that by changing the beginning of a word, you make a new word. By knowing how to spell word families you can build many different words. Look at the words in the *ake* family. By knowing that *a-k-e* spells /āk/, you can spell all these words.

Read the words in the *ake* family one column at a time. Then have the students read and spell the words with you.

Introduce the words in the *ame* family using the same steps.

1. Say the sound /ām/ and ask students what letters make the sound.
2. Say the letters *a-m-e* and ask students what sound they make.
3. Say the word *name* and ask students what letters spell /ām/ and what letter spells /n/.
4. Say the word *name* and ask students what letters spell *name*.

Use the same steps with the words in the *ade*, *ate*, and *ape* families. Emphasize that by changing the beginning of words in these families, you make new words.

When you get to the word *ate*, point out that it has a homonym. The number *eight* was a Book 1 sight word. Review the term *homonym*. After you have completed the last word family list, read aloud the words in the five lists. Ask students to identify the words which contain two or more syllables as you are reading. Refer to the Introduction to Book 1 if students need more practice hearing syllables.

❷ Writing Words

Instruct students to write the words that you dictate, which are found on the replica of the student page. Say each word, use it in a phrase or simple sentence, and say the word again.

❸ Dictionary Skills: Alphabetizing

Before introducing this exercise, be sure your students know the sequence of the alphabet and which letters are vowels. You may want students to write the alphabet on an index card or piece of paper and tape it to the inside cover of their books.

This exercise reviews alphabetizing words by the first two or three letters. Book 1 of this series has many exercises which help students to develop this skill. If a student is having trouble alphabetizing, follow the suggestions in the Introduction to Book 1.

❹ Using Sight Words

If students do not already know this saying, have them memorize it.

❺ Finding a Pattern

Do the first one or two items in this exercise as a group to make sure students understand what is required. Go over the words that they underline to make sure that they have found all the long *a* words before they answer the questions.

6 **Adding -ed and -ing to Verbs.** We add -ed to regular verbs (action words) to show action which happened in the past. We add -ing to show action which goes on over a period of time. When a word ends in a silent e, the final e is dropped before adding -ed or -ing. Add -ed and -ing to the verbs below. The first one has been done to get you started.

Verb	-ed	-ing
1. trade	traded	trading
2. name	named	naming
3. brake	braked	braking
4. tape	taped	taping
5. state	stated	stating

7 **Finding Another Pattern.** In Exercise 5 you learned that the final silent e is dropped from a word when -ed or -ing is added to it.

Fill in the blanks in the chart below to discover the rest of this pattern. The first one has been done to get you started.

Word	Root	Ending	Was e Dropped?
1. wading	wade	ing	yes
2. paved	pave	ed	yes
3. saving	save	ing	yes
4. shaker	shake	er	yes
5. traded	trade	ed	yes
6. shapeless	shape	less	no
7. safety	safe	ty	no
8. games	game	s	no
9. paleness	pale	ness	no
10. pavement	pave	ment	no

6   Lesson 1

6 **Adding -ed and -ing to Verbs**

This exercise serves two purposes. It provides the basis for the discovery of Silent e Pattern 1 which follows. It also introduces the concept of the principal parts of verbs. You may want to reinforce this by using the example words in short sentences.

Additional Activity:

Have students write sentences using the past tense and present participles formed in Exercise 6. This will reinforce the concept of how these forms are used.

7 **Finding Another Pattern**

This exercise builds on Exercise 6 and continues the discovery of Silent e Pattern 1. Be sure your students know what root words are and how to find them. If students have trouble with this, do a few with them as a group.

8 **Silent *e* Pattern 1.** Look at the endings in Exercise 7 and fill in the missing words below to state a pattern.

The silent *e* at the end of a word is dropped when we add an ending starting with a ___vowel___ .
(consonant *or* vowel)

The silent *e* is not dropped if the ending starts with a ___consonant___ .
(consonant *or* vowel)

9 **Using Words.** Fill in the blanks in the story with one of the words below. Use each word only once.

ate	cake	lemonade	shade
awake	games	paper	state
baked	later	parade	waded

After the ___parade___ , the Slade family went to the ___state___ park for a picnic. They found a table in the ___shade___ and unpacked the food and ___paper___ plates. The children ___waded___ in the stream and played ___games___ until it was time to eat. They ___ate___ hot dogs, salad, and a ___cake___ that Mrs. Slade had ___baked___ the day before. They also had ___lemonade___ to drink. ___Later___ , as darkness fell, the children who were still ___awake___ watched a fireworks display.

10 **Writing Sentences.** On the lines below, write the sentences that you hear.

1. ___Don't blame Jake because he was late.___
2. ___Mrs. Ames hated taking down the drapes.___
3. ___Jim is going to be in a parade in March.___
4. ___The baby was wakeful and didn't take a nap.___
5. ___The frame shop went up in flames last January.___
6. ___James was scraping the plates when we came by.___

Lesson 1   7

8 Silent *e* Pattern 1

Go over students' answers to Exercise 7 before having them fill in the blanks in this exercise. If they have done Exercise 7 correctly, they should have no trouble formulating and understanding this pattern.

9 Using Words

This exercise gives students a chance to see and use their word family words in context. Suggest that students check off each word as they use it, so that the process of elimination will help them find the answers. When they have filled in all the answers, have them read the entire paragraph for comprehension.

10 Writing Sentences

Instruct students to write the sentences that you dictate, which are on the replica of the student page. For the first few lessons, you may need to read some sentences twice. Encourage students to listen to the entire sentence and repeat it to themselves before they begin to write. This strategy will help them to develop their auditory memories.

Contractions were presented in Book 1 of this series. You may want to review how they are formed before beginning this dictation exercise. Note any specific errors. Design additional sentences, words, or phrases for specific problems.

Patterns found in these sentences include:
—contractions (1 and 4)
—Silent *e* Pattern 1 (2, 4, and 6)
—adding -*s* or -*es* (2, 5, and 6)

Lesson 2

The Word Families *ane, ale, ave, afe,* and *age*

Objectives

- **Word Families:** Learn to spell words in the *ane, ale, ave, afe,* and *age* families.
- **Sight Words:** Learn to spell *July, August, September, October, November,* and *December*. Use all 12 months to complete sentences.
- **Dictionary Skills:** Find abbreviations for the months in the dictionary.
  Find the past tense, past participle, and present participle forms for certain irregular verbs.
- **Writing Dates:** Learn to write dates three different ways.
- **Pattern:** Review the final silent *e* which makes a vowel long. Discover that aCe usually produces a long *a*.
- **Writing Sentences:** Practice writing word family and sight words in context.

Sight Words

Teach the sight words using the methods described on pages 9-12 in the introduction to this book.

❶ Listening

Introduce the words in the *ane* family using the following steps.

1. Say the sound /ān/ and ask students what letters make the sound.
2. Say the letters *a-n-e* and ask students what sound they make.
3. Say the word *cane* and ask students what letters spell /ān/ and what letter spells /k/.
4. Say the word *cane* and ask students what letters spell *cane*.

Point out that by changing the beginning of the words in each family, you can make new words.

Follow the same steps to introduce the words in the *ale, ave, afe,* and *age* families.

Point out some of the consonant blends in the representative family words, such as *pl* in *plane, sc* in *scale,* and *st* in *stage*. Consonant blends and digraphs are dealt with in detail in Book 3 of this series, so don't worry if students have trouble with them. You do not need to hold students responsible for all of these representative words. The longer words are included to let students know that many words contain these families. However, students gain confidence and have a sense of accomplishment when they are able to spell words with more than one syllable. Use your own judgment to decide whether students will be challenged or frustrated by the more difficult words.

Additional Activity:

Have students who need practice with segmentation skills write the number of syllables they hear in the two- and three-syllable word family words.

Lesson 2

The Word Families *ane, ale, ave, afe,* and *age*

Sight Words

July	September	November
August	October	December

Word Families

❶ Listening

ane

Listen to the sound *ane* makes in these words.

cane	vane	lane
Jane	sane	plane
mane	insane	airplane

ale

Listen to the sound *ale* makes in these words.

ale	scale	male
pale	sale	female
tale	salesperson	inhale

ave

Listen to the sound *ave* makes in these words.

cave	pave	brave	behave
gave	save	grave	forgave

afe

Listen to the sound *afe* makes in these words.

safe	safety	safely	chafe

age

Listen to the sound *age* makes in these words.

cage	age	page	engage
wage	teenager	stage	engagement

8   Lesson 2

2 Writing Words. On the lines below, write the words that you hear.

1. safe
2. sane
3. wage
4. sale
5. behave
6. stage
7. lane
8. brave
9. inhale
10. plane
11. safely
12. engage

3 Using Sight Words. Fill in the correct months in the sentences below. Use each of the 12 months once.

1. The United States celebrates its birthday in ___July___.
2. The shortest month is ___February___.
3. Yom Kippur is observed in September or ___October___.
4. Memorial Day is celebrated in ___May___.
5. Spring arrives in ___March___.
6. Christmas is celebrated in ___December___.
7. Martin Luther King's birthday is celebrated in ___January___.
8. Thanksgiving is celebrated in ___November___.
9. Labor Day is celebrated in ___September___.
10. ___August___ is the last full month of summer.
11. ___June___ is considered the wedding month.
12. Income tax must be paid by the 15th of ___April___.

4 Dictionary Skills: Abbreviations. Write the abbreviations for the following months on the lines provided. Use your dictionary if necessary.

1. January ___Jan.___
2. February ___Feb.___
3. March ___Mar.___
4. April ___Apr.___
5. August ___Aug.___
6. September ___Sep. or Sept.___
7. October ___Oct.___
8. November ___Nov.___
9. December ___Dec.___

Lesson 2   9

2 Writing Words

Instruct students to write the words that you dictate, which are found on the replica of the student page. Say each word, use it in a phrase or simple sentence, and say the word again.

3 Using Sight Words

Students should write the name of the correct month in the blank in each sentence. If students don't know which month certain holidays come in, encourage them to find the information by using their dictionaries or a calendar. Tell them to use each month only once.

Additional Activity:

Have students write the saying they learned in Lesson 1 for remembering the number of days in each month.

4 Dictionary Skills: Abbreviations

Have students write the standard abbreviations for the months listed. Point out that *May*, *June*, and *July* are not normally abbreviated. *March* and *April* often are not abbreviated as well.

Dictionaries may vary on which abbreviations they list, and also on where they list them. If your students are not all using the same dictionary, help them to find these abbreviations and discuss variations, if necessary.

5 **Dictionary Skills: Irregular Verbs.** Some verbs (action words) do not have *-ed* added to show past time. If a verb does not have *-ed* added to show past time, it is called an irregular verb. The dictionary will usually list the past tense of irregular verbs after the listing for the present tense. Look at the examples below.

come (kŭm) *v.* **came** (kām), **come, com·ing.**

eat (ēt) *v.* **ate** (āt), **eat·en** (ēt′n), **eat·ing.**

The main entry is the present tense form of the verb. The second word is its past tense. The third word is the *past participle*, which is the form used with *have, has,* or *had.* The fourth word is the *present participle*, which is the *-ing* form of the verb.

Below are examples of how these different forms are used in sentences.

1. Please *come* over and *eat* pizza with us.	(Present Tense)
2. Jake *came* over and *ate* with us last night.	(Past Tense)
3. He has *eaten* with us many times.	(Past Participle)
4. We have *eaten* together every Friday.	(Past Participle)
5. Jane had *eaten* with us once or twice.	(Past Participle)
6. I am *coming* over tonight.	(Present Participle)
7. You are *coming* with us, aren't you?	(Present Participle)
8. She is *coming* with us tonight.	(Present Participle)
9. He was *coming* to visit us.	(Present Participle)
10. They were *coming* to see the play.	(Present Participle)

Look up the following irregular verbs in the dictionary and write the different forms on the lines provided. The first one has been done to get you started.

Present Tense	Past Tense	*Have, Has,* or *Had* + Verb	*-ing* Form of Verb
1. make	made	made	making
2. shake	shook	shaken	shaking
3. become	became	become	becoming
4. take	took	taken	taking
5. wake	woke	waked *or* woken	waking
6. give	gave	given	giving

10　Lesson 2

5 Dictionary Skills: Irregular Verbs

Many irregular verbs have one or more principal parts with long vowel sounds. Because they are irregular, the differences in spelling among the principal parts can cause confusion. Take plenty of time to introduce the concept of irregular verbs. Help students to find the listings in their dictionaries. Most dictionaries list the principal parts of irregular verbs directly after the pronunciation guide. The principal parts of regular verbs generally are not listed.

Introduce the terms *past participle* and *present participle*, but don't insist that students learn them. Be sure, however, that they understand how these two forms are used. Go over the example sentences and develop additional ones, if necessary. Then have students complete the exercise on their own.

Additional Activities:

Have students create oral sentences using the principal parts formed in Exercise 5. This will reinforce the concept of how these forms are used. Make this a group activity.

Have students start a table of irregular verbs in their notebooks. You might have them list the principal parts of all the irregular verbs presented in this text, or only the ones that they have trouble learning to spell.

6 **Writing Dates.** Here are three different ways to write the same date.

December 1, 1992   Dec. 1, 1992   12/1/92

Write each of the following dates in two other ways on the lines provided.

1. October 2, 1994   Oct. 2, 1994   10/2/94
2. Feb. 4, 1989   February 4, 1989   2/4/89
3. 4/21/59   April 21, 1959   Apr. 21, 1959
4. January 3, 1951   Jan. 3, 1951   1/3/51
5. Sept. 7, 1990   September 7, 1990   9/7/90
6. 11/12/66   November 12, 1966   Nov. 12, 1966

7 **Reviewing a Pattern.** Underline each word below that has a long *a* sound. Then make the long vowel mark (‾) over each long *a*.

cap	v̄ane	br̄ave	glad	gr̄ade	p̄ale	tap
sc̄ale	man	c̄ape	van	̄ape	l̄ate	J̄ane
w̄ade	Brad	mad	t̄ape	Jan	par̄ade	tr̄ade

C is a symbol which stands for any consonant. **V** stands for any vowel. Fill in the blank below to restate the pattern learned in Lesson 1.

Pattern: Words that end with a**C**e usually have a ___long___ *a* sound.
(long *or* short)

8 **Writing Sentences.** On the lines below, write the sentences that you hear.

1. How many sales did Dave make in July?
2. Mrs. Gale has taken her cane to be fixed.
3. The teenagers are saving their wages to buy a car.
4. By August Jane had become used to her new airplane.
5. James gave safety tips to Mr. Page's class in October.
6. Mr. Slade forgave me for making a mistake on that page.

Lesson 2   11

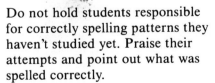

6 Writing Dates

Explain to students that in the United States dates are written in the order of month, day, and year, whether they are represented by words or abbreviations plus numbers, or by numbers alone. (You may want to point out that in many other countries the day is written before the month.)

If students are not already familiar with the form that uses only numbers, you may want to have them write out the names of the months in order and then number them.

7 Reviewing a Pattern

This exercise reviews the a**C**e pattern presented in Lesson 1. Be sure students understand that a bold capital **C** represents any consonant, and a bold capital **V** represents any vowel. These symbols will be used throughout this text.

8 Writing Sentences

Instruct students to write the sentences that you dictate, which are on the replica of the student page. Note any specific errors. Design additional sentences, words, or phrases for specific problems.

Do not hold students responsible for correctly spelling patterns they haven't studied yet. Praise their attempts and point out what was spelled correctly.

The possessive form of singular nouns was introduced in Book 1 of this series. You may want to review the *'s* before beginning this exercise.

Patterns found in these sentences include:
—irregular verb forms (2, 4, 5, and 6)
—adding *-s* or *-es* (1, 3, and 5)
—Silent *e* Pattern 1 (3, 4, 5, and 6)
—forming the possessive (5)

Lesson 3

The Word Families *ase*, *ace*, *aze*, *ange*, and *aste*

Objectives

- **Word Families:** Learn to spell words in the *ase*, *ace*, *aze*, *ange*, and *aste* families.
- **Sight Words:** Learn to spell *north*, *northern*, *east*, *eastern*, *south*, *southern*, *west*, and *western*.
  Learn to capitalize these words when they are used as proper names and use them to complete sentences.
- **Pattern:** Review Silent *e* Pattern 1.
- **Endings:** Add endings to words that end in silent *e*.
- **Alternative Spellings:** Learn that /ās/ can be spelled *ace* or *ase*, and that *ace* is a more common pattern.
- **Creating Sentences:** Write original sentences using word family and sight words.
- **Writing Sentences:** Practice writing word family and sight words in context.

Sight Words

Teach the sight words using the methods described on pages 9-12 in the introduction to this book.

Some people mispronounce the words ending with *ern*, saying /rĕn/ as the last syllable instead of /ĕrn/. This can lead to misspelling these words. Stress the correct pronunciation of these words with any students who have this difficulty.

❶ Listening

Introduce the words in the *ase* family using the following steps.

1. Say the sound /ās/ and ask students what letters make the sound in the first group of words.

2. Say the letters *a-s-e* and ask students what sound they make.
3. Say the word *base* and ask students what letters spell /ās/ and what letter spells /b/.
4. Say the word *base* and ask students what letters spell *base*.

Point out that by changing the beginning of the words in each family, you can make new words.

Follow the same steps to introduce the words in the *ace*, *aze*, *ange*, and *aste* families.

Point out some of the common blends in the representative word family words, such as *sp* in *space*, *gr*

in *graceful*, and *br* in *bracelet*. Make sure students can hear both consonant sounds in each blend. Contrast these blends with the digraph *ch* in *chase* and *change*, which makes one sound.

Additional Activity:

Have students who need to improve their segmentation skills write the number of syllables they hear in some of the two- and three-syllable word family and sight words.

Lesson 3

The Word Families *ase*, *ace*, *aze*, *ange*, and *aste*

Sight Words			
north	east	south	west
northern	eastern	southern	western

Word Families

ase

ace

aze

ange

aste

❶ Listening

Listen to the sound *ase* makes in these words.

base	case	vase
basement	chase	eraser

Listen to the sound *ace* makes in these words.

face	lace	pace	race
space	place	graceful	bracelet
trace	misplace	disgrace	

Listen to the sound *aze* makes in these words.

daze	haze	blaze	amaze
gaze	maze	craze	amazement

Listen to the sound *ange* makes in these words.

range	change	strange	danger
arrange	exchange	stranger	dangerous

Listen to the sound *aste* makes in these words.

haste	paste	taste	waste

2 **Writing Words.** On the lines below, write the words that you hear.

1. _taste_ 5. _case_ 9. _paste_
2. _base_ 6. _range_ 10. _facing_
3. _daze_ 7. _spaces_ 11. _grace_
4. _lace_ 8. _chase_ 12. _danger_

3 **Using Sight Words.** When the sight words in this lesson are used to indicate a direction, they are not capitalized. However, when they are used in geographical names, such as the names of cities, states, countries, continents, or parts of the world, they are usually capitalized. Study the examples below.

a *north* wind	*North* Dakota
the *east* side of town	*East* Africa
southern hospitality	the *South* Pacific
the *western* frontier	*Western* Sahara

Now fill in the blanks in the sentences below with one of the sight words from this lesson. Use capital letters when necessary.

1. The sun rises in the _east_ and sets in the _west_.
2. Herds of buffalo used to roam the _western_ states.
3. Mexico is _south_ of the Texas border.
4. Asia is often called "the Far _East_."
5. Alabama and Georgia are _southern_ states.
6. Massachusetts is on the _eastern_ seaboard.
7. Canada is _north_ of the United States.
8. The _Northern_ Hemisphere is north of the equator.
9. There is a wall dividing East and _West_ Berlin.
10. The Civil War was fought between the _North_ and the _South_.

Lesson 3   13

2 Writing Words

Instruct students to write the words that you dictate, which are found on the replica of the student page. Say each word, use it in a phrase or simple sentence, and say the word again.

3 Using Sight Words

Not all dictionaries and other sources agree on when these words should be capitalized. However, a good rule of thumb is to capitalize them if they are part of a proper name.

Go over the examples with students and provide others, if necessary. Encourage them to use their dictionaries in completing the exercise, but remind them that dictionaries will not always agree. Note that *North* and *South* are generally capitalized in the context of the Civil War, as in number 10.

4 **Reviewing a Pattern.** In Lesson I you discovered that the final silent *e* is dropped when an ending starting with a vowel is added. The silent *e* is not dropped if the ending starts with a consonant. Add the endings above the columns to each of the root words listed below.

Root Word	-ed	-ing	-s	-less
1. name	named	naming	names	nameless
2. face	faced	facing	faces	faceless
3. flame	flamed	flaming	flames	flameless
4. base	based	basing	bases	baseless
5. blame	blamed	blaming	blames	blameless
6. taste	tasted	tasting	tastes	tasteless
7. shape	shaped	shaping	shapes	shapeless
8. age	aged	aging	ages	ageless

5 **The Word Families *ace* and *ase*.** Write each word your teacher dictates in the correct column below.

	ace		ase
1.	face	1.	base
2.	pace	2.	case
3.	place	3.	chase
4.	race	4.	erase
5.	trace	5.	vase

Because the *ace* and *ase* family words rhyme, you will need to remember if the /s/ sound in a word is made by *c* or *s*. The *ace* spelling is more common. The five words you just wrote in the *ase* column are the most common words spelled with *ase*. To help you remember them, try to make up a sentence or a rhyme which uses all five words.

4 **Reviewing a Pattern**

Review Silent *e* Pattern I with students before they do this exercise. Then check to be sure they have dropped the silent *e* from each word they wrote in the first two columns and retained it in the words they wrote in the last two columns.

5 **The Word Families *ace* and *ase***

Before beginning this exercise, discuss with your students the problem presented by the *ace* and *ase* families. Point out that this problem is one that faces everyone who is learning to spell, and that others have learned to spell words in these two families.

Emphasize that reading helps people to become familiar with the way these words are spelled. The goal is to become familiar with these words, so that they will not have to think about whether *case* belongs to the *ase* or *ace* family.

Explain that you will be dictating five words from each of the families and that they should write the words under the correct heading. Then dictate the words on the replica of the student page in random order.

If a student has trouble with any of the words, they should be treated as sight words and added to the personal spelling list.

Encourage students to develop a mnemonic device for remembering the *ase* words. Remind them that there are fewer words that follow this pattern. Knowing this will help them to use probability in predicting the spelling of words not yet studied.

6 Creating Sentences. On a separate piece of paper, write five sentences about the picture below. Think about what the occasion is, what is happening in the picture, what each person is concerned about, and how things may end up. Use some of the following long *a* words in your sentences.

bake	came	chase	made
baker	place	danger	save
cake	vase	dangerous	safe
plate	arrange	amazement	safely

7 Writing Sentences. On the lines below, write the sentences that you hear.

1. Don't waste that paste.
2. I misplaced my eraser.
3. Mr. Granger was behaving strangely.
4. Grace was amazed by the stranger's gaze.
5. Jane is arranging poppies in the red vase.
6. Dave set the pace at the race in North Orange.
7. The southern states were blazing hot last August.
8. They use a safety net because that trick is dangerous.

Lesson 3   15

---

6 Creating Sentences

Before asking students to write their sentences, discuss the picture with them. This will help them to develop ideas for their sentences before trying to write them.

Students should have access to a dictionary as they write and should be encouraged to try to look up words they have difficulty with. Do not discourage them from using words that are troublesome. If students make errors trying to spell words they are not familiar with, discuss how to find those words in a dictionary.

Remember that errors in words that have not yet been studied should not be treated negatively. Find something to praise and take the time to point out what was done correctly.

7 Writing Sentences

Instruct students to write the sentences that you dictate, which are on the replica of the student page. Note any specific errors. Design additional sentences, words, or phrases for specific problems.

As the dictation sentences in this text get longer, you may want to have students write their dictation sentences in their notebooks or on separate sheets of paper.

Patterns found in these sentences include:
—alternative spellings for /$\bar{a}$s/ (2, 5, and 6)
—contractions (1)
—Silent *e* Pattern 1 (2, 3, 4, 5, 7, and 8)
—possession (4)
—capitalization of direction words (6)

Lesson 4

The Word Families *ail*, *aim*, *ain*, and *ait*

Objectives

- **Word Families:** Learn to spell words in the *ail*, *aim*, *ain*, and *ait* families.
- **Sight Words:** Learn to spell *people, person, talk, walk, lose, find, loose,* and *tight*. Learn a mnemonic device for distinguishing between *lose* and *loose*.
- **Word Building:** Add word families to initial consonants and blends.
- **Using Words in Context:** Complete a paragraph by filling in sight words.
- **Pattern:** Discover that *ai* usually produces long *a*.
- **Dictionary Skills:** Use the dictionary to determine homonym spellings based on context.
- **Creating Sentences:** Write an original story using word family and sight words.
- **Writing Sentences:** Practice writing word family and sight words in context.

Sight Words

Teach the sight words using the methods described on pages 9-12 in the introduction to this book.

Lesson 4

The Word Families *ail*, *aim*, *ain*, and *ait*

<table>
<tr><th colspan="4">Sight Words</th></tr>
<tr><td>people</td><td>talk</td><td>lose</td><td>loose</td></tr>
<tr><td>person</td><td>walk</td><td>find</td><td>tight</td></tr>
</table>

Word Families

ail

① Listening

Listen to the sound *ail* makes in these words.

ail	Gail	rail	tail
fail	pail	railroad	detail
mail	sail	trail	retail
nail	sailor	daily	tailor

aim

Listen to the sound *aim* makes in these words.

aim	claim	maim
aimless	reclaim	

ain

Listen to the sound *ain* makes in these words.

gain	pain	stain	remain
rain	plain	contain	maintain
train	complain	obtain	maintenance
strain	explain	retain	entertainment

ait

Listen to the sound *ait* makes in these words.

wait	waiter	trait	bait

16   Lesson 4

---

① Listening

Introduce the words in the *ail* family using the following steps.

1. Say the sound /āl/ and ask students what letters make the sound.
2. Say the letters *a-i-l* and ask students what sound they make.
3. Say the word *fail* and ask students what letters spell /āl/ and what letter spells /f/.
4. Say the word *fail* and ask students what letters spell *fail*.

Point out that by changing the beginning of the words in each family, you can make new words.

Follow the same steps to introduce the words in the *aim*, *ain*, and *ait* families.

Point out some of the common blends in the representative word family words, such as *cl* in *claim* and *tr* in *trail, train,* and *trait*. Make sure students can hear both consonant sounds in each blend.

❷ Writing Words. On the lines below, write the words that you hear.

1. _____sail_____   5. _____pain_____   9. _____Spain_____
2. _____main_____   6. _____mailing_____   10. _____railroad_____
3. _____waiting_____   7. _____bait_____   11. _____explain_____
4. _____claim_____   8. _____remain_____   12. _____aimless_____

❸ Word Building. Add either *ail*, *aim*, *ain*, or *ait* to each of the consonants to make a word.

1. b_ait_____   5. m_ain_____   9. cl_aim_____
2. f_ail_____   6. n_ail_____   10. gr_ain_____
3. g_ain_____   7. r_ail_____   11. pl_ain_____
4. h_ail_____   8. s_ail_____   12. tr_ail_____

❹ Using Sight Words

Part A. The spellings of the sight words *lose* and *loose* are often confused. One way to tell them apart is to remember that each word has an opposite that has the same number of letters.

1. The opposite of *lose* is *find*. Each word has __four__ letters.

2. The opposite of *loose* is *tight*. Each word has __five__ letters.

Part B. Write the correct sight word in each blank. Use each word only once.

Eight _____people_____ waited at the bus stop. When the bus came it was so crowded that one _____person_____ decided to _____walk_____. The other seven got on even though it was a _____tight_____ squeeze. No one could _____find_____ a seat. Two students standing in the aisle began to _____talk_____. "Would you check to see that the strap on my backpack isn't too _____loose_____?" asked one. The other replied, "Let me tighten it for you. You are about to _____lose_____ it."

Lesson 4   17

❷ Writing Words

Instruct students to write the words that you dictate, which are found on the replica of the student page. Say each word, use it in a phrase or simple sentence, and say the word again. Check to be sure students have capitalized *Spain* in number 9.

❸ Word Building

Instruct students to try each of the word families with each of the consonants or blends to determine which ones form words. When the consonant plus the word family makes a word, they should write the word family in the blank. Go over the first one with them. Help them to see that both *ail* and *ait* can be added to *b* to form words. Ask them if adding *aim* or *ain* to *b* would make a word. Encourage them to complete the exercise on their own.

The answers given on the replica of the student page are examples. Accept all correctly spelled words.

❹ Using Sight Words

In Part A of this exercise, students discover a mnemonic device for discriminating between *lose* and *loose*. Part B gives students a chance to use the sight words in context. When they have filled in all the words, have them read the entire paragraph for comprehension.

5 **Finding a Pattern.** In each pair of words, underline the word that has a long vowel sound.

1. man	<u>main</u>	4. pal	<u>pail</u>	7. <u>brain</u>	bran
2. am	<u>aim</u>	5. <u>rain</u>	ran	8. bat	<u>bait</u>
3. <u>plain</u>	plan	6. <u>claim</u>	clam	9. van	<u>vain</u>

What letter has been added in the underlined words to make the *a* long? __i__

Where has the letter been added? _____ after the a _____

Can you hear the added letter in the underlined words? __no__

What sound does *ai* make in the words above? long a *or* ā

Pattern: The letters *ai* usually make the long *a* sound.

6 **Dictionary Skills: Homonyms.** *Homonyms* are words that sound alike. The families *ain* and *ane* and the families *ail* and *ale* have some homonym pairs that can easily be confused. To select the correct spelling, you must know the meaning of the word. A dictionary can help you choose the correct word from a pair of homonyms. Answer the following questions using a dictionary when you need to.

1. Is a boy a *mail* or a *male*? _____ male
2. Which hurts, a *pain* or a *pane*? _____ pain
3. Which shows the direction of the wind, a *vain* or a *vane*? _____ vane
4. Does a clipper ship have *sails* or *sales*? _____ sails
5. Which flies, a *plain* or a *plane*? _____ plane
6. Is a story a *tail* or a *tale*? _____ tale
7. Does a lion have a *main* or a *mane*? _____ mane
8. Is a light color *pail* or *pale*? _____ pale
9. Which is a drink, *ail* or *ale*? _____ ale
10. Which is icy, *hail* or *hale*? _____ hail

18   Lesson 4

5 **Finding a Pattern**

Students should work independently on this exercise. Check to be sure they have underlined the correct words.

Point out that *ai* usually makes the long *a* sound. You may want to mention some common exceptions, such as *again*, *certain*, and *mountain*.

6 **Dictionary Skills: Homonyms**

While homonyms can have the same spelling, we are primarily interested in those that are spelled differently. Students will already be familiar with many of these homonyms, so they won't have to look up their definitions. However, they should look up any they are unsure of. Stress the fact that knowing the meaning of the word is the only sure way of spelling a homonym correctly.

Additional Activity:

Alternative spellings of long vowels result in many pairs of homonyms. If students have particular trouble with alternative spellings of homonyms, you might suggest that they set aside a special section of their notebooks where they can list homonyms and their definitions. They should review their lists periodically and be quizzed on these words.

7 **Creating Sentences.** On a separate piece of paper, write a story about these pictures. Use some of the following long *a* words in your sentences.

Gail	wait	later	date
sail	mail	railing	gave
sailor	daily	came	exclaim

Sept. 15   Oct. 2   Dec. 20

8 **Writing Sentences.** On the lines below, write the sentences that you hear.

1. I like to walk in the rain.

2. They are taking a train through the western plains.

3. Can you name an animal that has a mane and a tail?

4. Gail talked to the person who claimed to have her mail.

5. The waiter complained that the people didn't give him a tip.

6. The details of the sailor's face were engraved on Jane's mind.

Lesson 4   19

---

7 **Creating Sentences**

Before students begin writing, discuss the illustrations in class to help them develop some ideas to write about. You may also want to talk with them about style and tone. Do they want to be serious? Dramatic? Melodramatic? Let students enjoy this exercise.

Remember that students should not be held responsible for words they have not yet studied. We feel that it is acceptable for students to make phonetically correct misspellings of words they have not yet studied. If you choose to correct them, be supportive of their attempts.

8 **Writing Sentences**

Instruct students to write the sentences that you dictate, which are on the replica of the student page. Note any specific errors. Design additional sentences, words, or phrases for specific problems.

Sentence 3 is a question. You may want to review the use of question marks before beginning the dictation.

Patterns found in these sentences include:
—homonyms (2, 3, and 4)
—Silent *e* Pattern 1 (2 and 6)
—adding -*s* or -*es* (2 and 6)
—questions (3)
—contractions (5)
—possession (6)

Lesson 5

The Word Families *aid*, *air*, *aise*, and *aint*

Objectives

- **Word Families:** Learn to spell words in the *aid*, *air*, *aise*, and *aint* families.
- **Sight Words:** Learn to spell *waist*, *faith*, *add*, *odd*, *pretty*, *beauty*, *every*, and *direction*.
- **Homonyms:** Learn to discriminate between *waste* and *waist*.
- **Dictionary Skills:** Use the dictionary to find the correct spelling of words that end in aCe and aiC.
- **Familiar Sayings:** Complete some familiar sayings by filling in long *a* words.
  Tell what one of the sayings means.
- **Writing Sentences:** Practice writing word family and sight words in context.
- **Creating Sentences:** Use designated word family words in original sentences.

Sight Words

Teach the sight words using the methods described on pages 9-12 in the introduction to this book. Point out that *waist* and *faith*, like the word family words in this lesson, use *ai* to spell long *a*.

❶ Listening

Introduce the words in the *aid* family using the following steps.

1. Say the sound /ād/ and ask students what letters make the sound.
2. Say the letters *a-i-d* and ask students what sound they make.
3. Say the word *laid* and ask students what letters spell /ād/ and what letter spells /l/.
4. Say the word *laid* and ask students what letters spell *laid*.

Point out that by changing the beginning of the words in each family, you can make new words.

Follow the same steps to introduce the words in the *air*, *aise*, and *aint* families.

When you come to the *aise* family, point out that the *s* is pronounced /z/.

The *cqu* combination in *acquaint* and *acquaintance* is very difficult. Note that *q* is followed by *u* in English words and that the *c* is silent in these words. You do not need to hold students responsible for spelling these words correctly.

❷ Writing Words

Instruct students to write the words that you dictate, which are found on the replica of the student page. Say each word, use it in a phrase or simple sentence, and say the word again.

The Word Families *aid*, *air*, *aise*, and *aint*

Sight Words			
waist	add	pretty	every
faith	odd	beauty	direction

Word Families	
aid	
air	
aise	
aint	

❶ Listening

Listen to the sound *aid* makes in these words.

aid	maid	raid
laid	paid	braid
afraid	prepaid	braided

Listen to the sound *air* makes in these words.

air	pair	hair	flair
fair	repair	chair	stairs

Listen to the sound *aise* makes in these words.

raise	appraise	mayonnaise
praise	appraisal	

Listen to the sound *aint* makes in these words.

faint	restraint	acquaint
paint	complaint	acquaintance

❷ Writing Words. On the lines below, write the words that you hear.

1. chair
2. raise
3. aid
4. pair
5. faint
6. paid
7. hair
8. raid
9. complaint
10. appraise
11. upstairs
12. painting

20   Lesson 5

---

3 **Homonyms: *Waste* and *Waist*.** Look up *waste* and *waist* in the dictionary and write their definitions below.

waste ___to use or consume carelessly or needlessly; squander___

waist ___the part of the body between the rib cage and the pelvis___

Now write either *waste* or *waist* in the sentences below.

1. The slacks had patch pockets and a belted ___waist___.

2. Do you know what the saying, Haste makes ___waste___, means?

3. Jane went on a diet and took two inches off her ___waist___.

4. Grace didn't want to ___waste___ any yarn, so she made mittens with what was left.

4 **Dictionary Skills: Finding the Correct Spelling.** You have learned that there are two common spelling patterns that represent the long *a* sound: aCe and aiC. A dictionary can help you choose the correct spelling for words that end in the sound /āC/.

Each of the words spelled phonetically below contains the long *a* sound. Use the dictionary to find the correct spelling based on the meaning given. Look first for the aCe pattern; then for aiC. When you find the spelling that matches the meaning, write the word in the appropriate column below. The first one has been done to get you started.

Phonetic Spelling	Meaning	aCe	aiC
1. /sān/	having a healthy mind	*sane*	_____
2. /lō′ kāt/	to find where something is	locate	_____
3. /grāp/	a fruit that grows on vines in bunches	grape	_____
4. /rĕ mān′/	to stay in a place	_____	remain
5. /trāl/	a path for hikers	_____	trail
6. /plān/	tool used to make wood smooth	plane	_____
7. /rĕ pār′/	to fix something that was broken	_____	repair
8. /flār/	a natural talent for doing something	_____	flair

Lesson 5   21

---

3 **Homonyms: *Waste* and *Waist***

Encourage students to put the definitions into their own words.

4 **Dictionary Skills: Finding the Correct Spelling**

Before beginning this exercise, remind students that letters between double slashes, e.g. /sān/, represent sounds or pronunciations rather than spellings. Therefore, a phonetic spelling represents the way the word is pronounced.

In this exercise students learn to look for more than one possible spelling and to determine the correct spelling based on the meaning of the word. The meanings in the text will not match those in the dictionary exactly, so students will need to compare the meaning in the text with the dictionary's definition and then decide if it is a match.

Go over the first one as a group so that students will understand what is required. If necessary, do the next one or two together as well.

Additional Activity:

Have students use the words in sentences of their own.

5 **Familiar Sayings.** Fill in the blanks in these familiar sayings with the long *a* words below.

gained   hesitates   safe   tale   waste

1. ____Waste____ not, want not.
2. Better ____safe____ than sorry.
3. He who ____hesitates____ is lost.
4. Nothing ventured, nothing ____gained____.
5. That is just an old wives' ____tale____.

Now select one of the sayings above and write what it means in your own words.

____Answers will vary.____

____

____

____

6 **Writing Sentences.** On the lines below, write the sentences that you hear.

1. ____The mayonnaise had an odd taste.____
2. ____Gail braids her sister's hair once in a while.____
3. ____Kate had a flair for painting pretty portraits.____
4. ____Every complaint they raised was exaggerated.____
5. ____Every detail of the painting added to its beauty.____
6. ____When James repaired the stairs, he added a railing.____
7. ____Mrs. Granger was afraid her maid would be late.____
8. ____Jane had faith in the directions Dale had given her.____

22   Lesson 5

5 **Familiar Sayings**

When students have completed the exercise, discuss the meanings of the various sayings.

Additional Activity:

Have students think of other sayings that have long *a* words in them.

6 **Writing Sentences**

Instruct students to write the sentences that you dictate, which are on the replica of the student page. Note any specific errors. Design additional sentences, words, or phrases for specific problems.

Sentence 5 contains the possessive pronoun *its*. The difference between *its* and the contraction *it's* will be covered later in this series. Do not hold students responsible for being able to spell correctly patterns they haven't yet studied.

Patterns found in these sentences include:
—possession (2)
—adding *-s* or *-es* (2, 3, 6, and 8)
—*aCe/aiC* spellings (3 and 6)
—Silent *e* Pattern 1 (4)
—irregular verb forms (8)

7 **Creating Sentences.** Read the following story.

> Dave and Blain have a shop where they make and repair furniture. Dave is a fine craftsman who enjoys working with his hands, knows the tools of his trade, and appreciates the beauty of wood. Blain has a flair for numbers and is good with people. He manages the business and waits on the customers who come to the shop.

On the lines below, write about what might happen in their shop on an ordinary day. Use some form of each word below in a sentence.

1. chair _____
_____

2. repair _____
_____

3. paint _____
_____

4. flair _____
_____

5. paid _____
_____

6. prepaid _____
_____

7. complaint _____
_____

8. praise _____
_____

Lesson 5   23

7 ## Creating Sentences

Discuss the situation with students before they begin to write. Have them imagine the details of the shop and suggest some possible incidents which might occur in a typical day. Encourage them to use as many long *a* and sight words in their sentences as they can.

If students ask how to spell a word that they have not yet studied, encourage them to look it up in the dictionary. Remember that errors in words that haven't yet been studied shouldn't be treated negatively.

Point out any parts of the word that are spelled correctly and praise the effort.

Lesson 6

The Word Families *ay, are, ary*, and *azy*

Objectives

- **Word Families:** Learn to spell words in the *ay, are, ary*, and *azy* families.
- **Sight Words:** Learn to spell *very, carry, marry, merry, berry,* and *ferry.*
  Learn to distinguish between the sight words and words that sound almost the same.
- **Dictionary Skills:** Learn several *air* and *are* homonym pairs.
- **Word Building:** Add word families to initial consonants and blends.
- **Hearing Syllables:** Identify the number of syllables in words.
- **Writing by Syllables:** Write dictated words one syllable at a time.
- **Days of the Week:** Review the names of and abbreviations for the days of the week.
- **Creating Sentences:** Use designated words in original sentences.
- **Writing Sentences:** Practice writing word family and sight words in context.

Sight Words

Teach the sight words using the methods described on pages 9-12 in the introduction to this book.

1 Listening

Introduce the words in the *ay* family using the following steps.

1. Say the sound /ā/ and ask students what letters make the sound in the first group of words.
2. Say the letters *a-y* and ask students what sound they make.
3. Say the word *day* and ask students what letters spell /ā/ and what letter spells /d/.

Lesson 6

The Word Families *ay, are, ary*, and *azy*

Sight Words		
very	marry	berry
carry	merry	ferry

Word Families

1 Listening

ay

Listen to the sound *ay* makes in these words.

day	pay	play	way
say	repay	display	away
okay	payday	delay	anyway
stay	payment	portray	highway

are

Listen to the sound *are* makes in these words.

bare	flare	fare	rare
care	share	welfare	silverware

ary

Listen to the sound *ary* makes in these words.

vary	library	literary	primary
scary	voluntary	necessary	secondary
solitary	vocabulary	temporary	imaginary

azy

Listen to the sound *azy* makes in these words.

lazy	hazy	crazy

24   Lesson 6

---

4. Say the word *day* and ask students what letters spell *day*.

Point out that by changing the beginning of the words in each family, you can make new words.

Follow the same steps to introduce the words in the *are, ary,* and *azy* families.

Because *are* and *ary*, as well as *air* in Lesson 5, contain r-controlled vowels, dictionaries usually will not show them as having long *a* sounds. However, these families have been included in this text because the vowel sounds are very close to the long *a* sound.

Point out the first *r* in *library*. This *r* often is not pronounced, and therefore the word is misspelled. Also note the two /s/ sounds in *necessary*. Point out that the first is spelled with a *c*, while the second is spelled *ss*.

Point out the *fl* blend in *flare* and contrast it to the *sh* digraph in *share*. Students should be able to hear two sounds in *fl* but only one in *sh*.

2 **Writing Words.** On the lines below, write the words that you hear.

1. care
2. lazy
3. anyway
4. library

5. say
6. crazy
7. today
8. shared

9. primary
10. payday
11. imaginary
12. vocabulary

3 **Dictionary Skills: Sight Words.** Five of the sight words in this lesson have homonyms or words that are almost homonyms. Answer the following questions by choosing the correct spelling based on the context. Use a dictionary to check your answers.

1. Is a type of fruit a *berry* or a *bury*? _____ berry _____

2. Do you ask someone to *marry* you or *merry* you? _____ marry _____

3. Is a boat that carries things a *fairy* or a *ferry*? _____ ferry _____

4. When it's below zero, is it *vary* cold or *very* cold? _____ very _____

5. When people are happy, are they *marry* or *merry*? _____ merry _____

4 **Dictionary Skills: Homonyms.** The *air* and *are* families have some homonym pairs. Fill in either *air* or *are* in the sentences below. Use your dictionary when you need to.

1. A h_are_ is usually larger than a rabbit.

2. It rained today, but tomorrow should be f_air_ and warmer.

3. Gail bought a new p_air_ of shoes last weekend.

4. Mrs. Blair told her little girl that it isn't polite to st_are_.

5. James seems to have a fl_air_ for music.

6. I have an appointment to get my h_air_ cut today.

7. Do you remember when bus f_are_ was twenty-five cents?

8. To get to Dale's apartment, you have to go up three flights of st_air_s.

Lesson 6   25

2 **Writing Words**

Instruct students to write the words that you dictate, which are found on the replica of the student page. Say each word, use it in a phrase or simple sentence, and say the word again.

3 **Dictionary Skills: Sight Words**

Dictionaries may show different pronunciations for these pairs of words, but they are often pronounced so much alike that it is hard to distinguish between them.

4 **Dictionary Skills: Homonyms**

Students should get used to looking words up in their dictionaries when they are unsure of the spelling. For this exercise, remind them to look first for the *air* spelling and then for the *are* spelling to find a definition that fits the context of the sentence.

Some students may not need to use the dictionary at all to complete this exercise. Others may look up nearly every word. If a student is not using the dictionary but is making mistakes, encourage the student to use the dictionary more often. Conversely, if a student is using the dictionary for every word, you might suggest that the student not rely on the dictionary quite so heavily.

❺ Word Building

Instruct students to try each word family with each of the consonants or blends to determine which ones form words. When the consonant plus the word family makes a word, they should write the word family in the blank. Encourage them to use all the word families at least once.

The answers given on the replica of the student page are examples. Accept all correctly spelled words.

❻ Hearing Syllables

The purpose of this exercise is to confirm that students have the ability to distinguish syllables in words. Read the words below at a normal pace and ask students to write down the number of syllables they hear.

1. became	7. okay
2. trade	8. necessary
3. teenager	9. scrape
4. awake	10. silverware
5. brain	11. January
6. entertainment	12. fascinate

If students are having difficulty hearing syllables, have them repeat words after you, emphasizing the syllable division, e.g., *be-came*. Remind them that each syllable is formed with a push of air from the lungs. Tapping the syllables on a desk or clapping the syllables provides reinforcement for some students.

❼ Writing Words by Syllables

Dictate each of these words by syllables, emphasizing the syllables. Then pronounce the whole word normally. Tell students to write the words syllable by syllable. Tell them that the number of blanks for each word indicates the number of syllables in that particular word. When they have written the word by

syllables, have them write the whole word on the line provided.

When students have finished the dictation, help them to pronounce the words by syllables.

Don't insist that students follow the conventional division of syllables. For instance, it doesn't matter if a student puts the second *n* in *mayonnaise* with the second or third syllable.

This exercise is in preparation for a study of syllable types and syllabication which begins in Unit 2. All of these words except the challenge

word are representative word family words in Unit 1.

Challenge words are included in some of these exercises to give students a sense of accomplishment and to help them gain confidence in their ability to predict the spelling of longer words. Praise whatever is correct in these attempts.

---

❺ **Word Building.** Add either *ay, are, ary,* or *azy* to each of the letters below to make a word.

1. b_ay_	4. l_azy_	7. cr_azy_
2. c_are_	5. m_ay_	8. gl_are_
3. d_ay_	6. v_ary_	9. gr_ay_

❻ **Hearing Syllables.** Write down the number of syllables in each of the words you hear.

1. _2_	4. _2_	7. _2_	10. _3_
2. _1_	5. _1_	8. _4_	11. _4_
3. _3_	6. _4_	9. _1_	12. _3_

❼ **Writing Words by Syllables.** Write the words that your teacher dictates one syllable at a time. Then write the whole word.

First Syllable	Second Syllable	Third Syllable	Fourth Syllable	Whole Word
1. mis	take			mistake
2. a	fraid			afraid
3. sail	or			sailor
4. lem	on	ade		lemonade
5. a	maze	ment		amazement
6. may	on	naise		mayonnaise
7. ex	ag	ger	ate	exaggerate
8. en	ter	tain	ment	entertainment

Challenge word:

co	or	di	nate	coordinate

8 **Reviewing the Days of the Week.** On the longer lines below, write the names of the days of the week, which you learned as sight words in Book 1. On the shorter lines, write an abbreviation for each day.

1. Sunday   Sun.
2. Monday   Mon.
3. Tuesday   Tues. *or* Tu.
4. Wednesday   Wed.
5. Thursday   Thurs. *or* Thur.
6. Friday   Fri.
7. Saturday   Sat.

9 **Creating Sentences.** On the lines below, write a sentence using each of the "day" words given.

1. today _____
2. yesterday _____
3. someday _____
4. birthday _____
5. holiday _____

10 **Writing Sentences.** On the lines below, write the sentences that you hear.

1. We were very lazy all day yesterday.
2. Will you carry the silverware over to the tray?
3. Gail made the last payment on her cars in February.
4. Gary said it was okay to stay and play the tapes.
5. It will be necessary to raise the train fare in January.
6. The repair Ray made on my chair was only temporary.
7. Mary wanted to vary the way she fixed her hair.
8. The fans were afraid that the games would be delayed.

Lesson 6   27

---

8 **Reviewing the Days of the Week**

The days of the week were sight words in Book 1 of this series. Be sure that any students who are starting in Book 2 can spell these words.

The abbreviations for the days of the week may vary according to the source used. Accept any abbreviation in general use.

9 **Creating Sentences**

As with other free writing exercises, if students ask how to spell a word that they have not studied, encourage them to look it up in the dictionary. Remember that errors in words that haven't been studied shouldn't be treated negatively. Point out any parts of the word that are spelled correctly and praise the effort.

10 **Writing Sentences**

Instruct students to write the sentences that you dictate, which are on the replica of the student page. Note any specific errors. Design additional sentences, words, or phrases for specific problems.

Patterns found in these sentences include:
—homonyms (1, 5, and 7)
—questions (2)
—irregular verb forms (3 and 6)
—adding -*s* or -*es* (4 and 8)

Review of Unit 1

The Long *a*

1 **Word Building.** Add one of the word families listed below to each of the consonants or blends to make a word. Do not make the same word twice.

ake	ape	afe	aze	aim	air	are
ame	ane	age	ange	ain	aise	ary
ade	ale	ase	aste	ait	aint	azy
ate	ave	ace	ail	aid	ay	

1. b_ake_____
2. d_ate_____
3. f_aint_____
4. f_ade_____
5. l_ane_____
6. m_ale_____
7. m_aze_____
8. n_ame_____
9. p_are_____
10. r_age_____
11. s_afe_____
12. s_ail_____
13. w_ait_____
14. w_are_____
15. cr_azy_____
16. dr_ape_____
17. fl_air_____
18. sp_ace_____

2 **Reviewing the Patterns for Spelling Long *a*.** On the lines below, write the words that you hear.

1. ___name_____
2. ___rail_____
3. ___taste_____
4. ___say_____
5. ___lazy_____

Five different ways to spell long *a* are used in the words above. Write another word for each of the five spellings for long *a*.

1. aCe _____
2. aiC _____
3. aCCe _____
4. ay _____
5. aCy _____

Review of Unit 1

The Long *a*

Objectives

- **Word Building:** Add word families to initial consonants and blends.
- **Patterns:** Review the patterns for spelling long *a*. Review Silent *e* Pattern 1.
- **Endings:** Add endings to words that end in silent *e* and to words that do not.
- **Dates:** Review the months by writing out dates.
- **Irregular Verbs:** Learn and review the principal parts of some irregular verbs.
- **Filling out Forms:** Fill out a form based on an imaginary incident.
- **Creating Sentences:** Describe an imaginary incident using given details.
- **Homonyms:** Review some aCe and aiC homonym pairs.
- **Writing Sentences:** Practice writing word family and sight words in context.
- **Puzzle:** Review long *a* family words and sight words by completing a crossword puzzle.

1 **Word Building**

Have students add one of the word families to each consonant or blend to make a word. Encourage students to use as many of the word families as they can in this exercise. However, there are more word families than there are consonants, so they will not be able to use them all.

The answers given on the replica of the student page are examples. Accept all correctly spelled words.

2 **Reviewing the Patterns for Spelling Long *a***

In this exercise, the following long *a* patterns are reviewed: aCe, aiC, aCCe, ay, and aCy.

3 **Reviewing a Pattern.** Fill in the blanks to review Silent *e* Pattern 1.

The silent *e* at the end of a word is dropped when an ending starting with a
___vowel___ is added. The silent *e* is not dropped when the ending
starts with a ___consonant___ .

4 **Adding Endings.** Add the endings to the words below. Drop the final
silent *e* when necessary.

1. pave + ment	pavement	11. shade + ed	shaded
2. trade + ing	trading	12. pain + less	painless
3. plain + ly	plainly	13. save + ing	saving
4. blame + ed	blamed	14. shape + less	shapeless
5. fate + ful	fateful	15. wait + ing	waiting
6. late + ness	lateness	16. main + ly	mainly
7. scrape + ing	scraping	17. inhale + ing	inhaling
8. behave + ior	behavior	18. shake + er	shaker
9. grade + ing	grading	19. care + less	careless
10. paint + er	painter	20. wake + ful	wakeful

5 **Writing Dates.** Write each of the dates below by spelling out the
month. Do not use abbreviations.

1. 1/3/51	January 3, 1951	7. 10/11/84	October 11, 1984
2. 12/1/79	December 1, 1979	8. 3/19/50	March 19, 1950
3. 5/6/90	May 6, 1990	9. 4/1/10	April 1, 1910
4. 8/2/45	August 2, 1945	10. 7/13/91	July 13, 1991
5. 2/25/89	February 25, 1989	11. 11/7/81	November 7, 1981
6. 9/15/92	September 15, 1992	12. 6/2/90	June 2, 1990

Review of Unit 1   29

3 **Reviewing a Pattern**

Since the **VCe** syllable pattern is
found throughout this text, it is
important to make sure students
have learned the rule for dropping
the final silent *e*.

4 **Adding Endings**

In this exercise, endings beginning
with vowels and with consonants
are added to both a**C**e words and
ai**C** and ai**CC** words. If necessary,
remind students that when endings
are added to ai**C** and ai**CC** words,
nothing is added or dropped from
the root word.

5 **Writing Dates**

This exercise reviews the spellings
of the months of the year and gives
students practice in translating from
the number of the month to its
name.

6 **Dictionary Skills: Irregular Verbs.** Write the irregular verb forms on the lines provided. Use your dictionary if necessary.

Present Tense	Past Tense	Have, Has, or Had + Verb	-ing Form of Verb
1. take	took	taken	taking
2. eat	ate	eaten	eating
3. forgive	forgave	forgiven	forgiving
4. say	said	said	saying
5. give	gave	given	giving
6. lay	laid	laid	laying
7. make	made	made	making
8. repay	repaid	repaid	repaying
9. become	became	become	becoming
10. shake	shook	shaken	shaking

7 **Filling out Forms.** Fill out the form on the next page using the following details. You can add other details if you wish.

Imagine that you operate a drill press in a factory. On January 3 there was a fire at the factory which began in the north corner of the large room that contains your drill press. No one was hurt in the fire, but the factory was closed for repairs for three weeks. It is now the first day of the next month, and you have to fill out a report for the insurance agency. The agency is trying to find out what caused the fire and wants to know what you saw. Before you left your drill press you saw:

- a woman run to the fire alarm and yell "Fire"
- a vat of wood stain catch on fire
- smoke quickly fill the room with haze
- a foreman wave his arms wildly at a maintenance man
- the maintenance man hit the sprinkler pipes with a long piece of wood
- water from the sprinkler pipes start to fall
- employees run to the exits on the east side of the building

30   Review of Unit 1

6 Dictionary Skills: Irregular Verbs

Several of these verbs (*forgive, say, lay, repay*) are being presented here for the first time. Allow students to use their dictionaries to look up the principal parts. Point out that *forgive, repay,* and *become* follow the same patterns as *give, pay,* and *come.*

If students began a table of irregular verbs in Lesson 2, have them add these to the list.

7 Filling out Forms

In Book 1 of this series, students developed a personal word list for filling out forms. They should refer to this list, if necessary, to fill out the top of this form. If students did not complete Book 1, have them add this personal information to their sight word list.

The details of the incident have been listed in the present tense deliberately. Students will have to restate these details by putting them in the past tense.

Discuss the incident with students before they write their reports. It may be helpful to draw a floor plan of the room, placing specific things such as the vat of wood stain. Remind students that they can add details of their own if they want to.

Insurance Report

Date: _____ Social Security Number: _____-____-_____

Name: _____ Date of Birth: _____
      Last   First   Middle   Mo./Day/Yr.

Address: _____
        Street   Apt. No.

   City   County   State   Zip Code

Phone: _____-_____-_____ Signature: _____
   (Area Code)

Description of Incident or Accident (Attach additional paper if necessary.)

_____

_____

_____

_____

_____

_____

_____

_____

_____

_____

_____

_____

_____

_____

_____

_____

_____

8 **Reviewing Homonyms.** Answer the following questions by selecting the spelling that fits the meaning.

1. Does a department store have *sales* or *sails*?   sales
2. Can you carry water in a *pale* or a *pail*?   pail
3. Does a belt go around your *waste* or your *waist*?   waist
4. Does a monkey have a *tale* or a *tail*?   tail
5. Is the glass in a window a *pane* or a *pain*?   pane
6. Does the postman deliver the *male* or the *mail*?   mail
7. Was a failed attempt in *vane* or in *vain*?   vain
8. If you are healthy, are you *hale* or *hail*?   hale
9. If you are sick, do you *ale* or *ail*?   ail
10. Is the charge for a bus ride the *fare* or the *fair*?   fare
11. When a fire burns, does it *flare* or *flair*?   flare
12. To go up one floor, do you climb the *stares* or the *stairs*?   stairs

9 **Writing Sentences.** On the lines below, write the sentences that you hear.

1. Trails went away from the cabin in every direction.
2. Gail was afraid Ray would lose his train fare.
3. The flames flared up and became a blaze.
4. Mrs. North said the kids behaved in a disgraceful way.
5. The children chased the chickens all over the place.
6. Will you carry this pail of paint over to the gate for me?
7. The salesperson forgot to give Jane her change.
8. It was plain that we should have taken the southern trail.

8 **Reviewing Homonyms**

This exercise reviews only one of each of these homonym pairs. If a student is having trouble with any of these, you may want to provide reinforcement activities that include both words.

9 **Writing Sentences**

Instruct students to write the sentences that you dictate, which are on the replica of the student page. Note any specific errors. Design additional sentences, words, or phrases for specific problems.

Patterns found in these sentences include:
—adding *-s* or *-es* (1, 3, 4, and 5)
—homonyms (2, 3, 6, and 8)
—Silent *e* Pattern 1 (3, 4, and 5)
—irregular verb forms (3, 4, 7, and 8)
—alternative spellings for /ās/ (4 and 5)

10 **Crossword Puzzle.** Use the clues below to complete this crossword puzzle. Most of the answers are word family or sight words from Unit 1.

¹D	E	C	E	²M	B	E	³R		⁴F	E	⁵B			
A				A			E		A		E			
N		⁶F	A	I	L		T		C		A			
G		A		L	⁷J	A	N		E		U			
E		I			⁸S		I				T			
⁹R	E	T	A	I	¹⁰N		¹¹L	A	T	E	L	Y		
O		H			E		A							
U		¹²F	A	S	C	I	N	A	T	E				
S		U			E		E							
		¹³L	O	O	S	E		¹⁴S	E	P	¹⁵T			
¹⁶P			S		¹⁷W		A			A				
¹⁸A	I	R	P	L	A	N	E	¹⁹A	G	E	S			
I			R		S		D			T				
²⁰R	E	P	L	A	Y		²¹D	A	T	E				

Across

1. The last month
4. Abbreviation for the second month
6. The opposite of succeed
7. Abbreviation for the first month
9. Keep; save; hold onto
11. Recently: Have you seen Jane ___?
12. To attract and hold the interest of someone
13. The opposite of tight
14. Abbreviation for the ninth month
18. The fastest way to travel is by ___.
19. Stages or period of time: the Middle ___
20. To play again
21. The day of the month: What is today's ___?

Down

1. Unsafe: It is ___ to play with matches.
2. What the post office delivers
3. The opposite of wholesale
4. Where your eyes, nose, and mouth are located
5. This is only skin deep.
6. Loyal: My dog is a ___ friend.
8. Fifty of these form the U.S.
10. Required or essential
15. To tell the flavor of
16. Two of a kind: a ___ of shoes
17. The opposite of east
19. The opposite of subtract

Review of Unit 1   33

---

10 **Crossword Puzzle**

Have students complete the crossword puzzle. Tell them that all the answer words are long *a* words or sight words from Unit 1. The clues are mostly definitions that rely on the students' general knowledge. If they have difficulty, you might want to have them work in pairs.

Allow them to use a dictionary if they want to. If necessary, give them the list of answer words that follows and have them check off words as they use them.

add	lately
ages	loose
airplane	mail
beauty	necessary
dangerous	pair
date	replay
December	retail
face	retain
fail	Sept.
faithful	states
fascinate	taste
Feb.	west
Jan.	

Unit 1 Tests

We recommend that you test your students on the word family and sight words from Unit 1 before going on. The following are suggested lists of representative word family words and sight words from Unit 1. You may wish to substitute other words to meet the needs of your students.

Dictate each word and use it in a simple sentence. Students should be able to spell 90 percent of these words correctly.

Family Words	Sight Words
1. fair	1. very
2. page	2. talk
3. made	3. lose
4. anyway	4. August
5. praise	5. add
6. baking	6. people
7. face	7. September
8. chase	8. northern
9. paid	9. beauty
10. change	10. April
11. taste	11. carry
12. state	12. southern
13. faint	13. loose
14. retail	14. berry
15. safety	15. February
16. welfare	16. western
17. became	17. waist
18. maintain	18. person
19. amazement	19. every
20. temporary	20. direction

Lesson 7

The Word Families *e*, *ee*, and *eer*

Objectives

- **Word Families:** Learn to spell words in the *e*, *ee*, and *eer* families.
- **Sight Words:** Learn to spell *move*, *prove*, *length*, *strength*, *special*, and *especially*.
- **Syllable Types:** Review closed (**CVC**), **Cl**e, and **VC**e syllable types. Learn the open syllable type.
- **Writing Sentences:** Practice writing word family and sight words in context.

Sight Words

Teach the sight words using the methods described on pages 9-12 in the introduction to this book. These sight words should be taught in pairs.

Point out to students that the *o* in *move* and *prove* makes an unusual sound for a single *o*, i.e., /o͞o/. Draw attention to *ength* in *length* and *strength*. Point out that *especially* is formed from the root word *special* with a prefix and suffix added.

❶ Listening

Introduce the words in the *e* family using the following steps.

1. Say the sound /ē/ and ask students what letter makes the sound in the first group of words.
2. Say the letter *e* and ask students what sound it makes.
3. Say the word *me* and ask students what letter spells /ē/ and what letter spells /m/.
4. Say the word *me* and ask students what letters spell *me*.

Explain that there are several ways to spell long *e*. This lesson presents two ways: *e* and *ee*.

Follow the same steps to introduce the words in the *ee* and *eer* families.

Because *eer* family words contain r-controlled vowels, many dictionaries will not show them as having long *e* sounds. However, the *eer* family is included here because the vowel sound is very close to the long *e* sound.

Point out the silent *k* in *knee*. Point out some common blends in the representative family words, such as *pr* in *prefix* and *fr* in *free* and

freedom. Be sure students can hear both consonant sounds in each blend.

❷ Writing Words

Instruct students to write the words that you dictate, which are found on the replica of the student page. Say each word, use it in a phrase or simple sentence, and say the word again.

Lesson 7

The Word Families *e*, *ee*, and *eer*

Sight Words		
move	length	special
prove	strength	especially

Word Families

e

❶ **Listening**

Listen to the sound *e* makes in these words.

me	ego	being	legal
be	equal	beyond	react
he	prefix	maybe	senior

ee

Listen to the sound *ee* makes in these words.

bee	tree	three	flee
fee	knee	agree	free
see	needle	coffee	freedom

eer

Listen to the sound *eer* makes in these words.

beer	cheer	pioneer
deer	steer	volunteer

❷ **Writing Words.** On the lines below, write the words that you hear.

1. tree
2. being
3. agree
4. steer
5. senior
6. maybe
7. pioneer
8. freedom
9. even

❸ Types of Syllables

Learning to recognize some of the most common types of syllables that form English words can give students more confidence in predicting the spelling of words they haven't studied and help to make them more independent spellers.

In this exercise, students discover the attributes of four common syllable types. Two of them, closed syllables and Cle syllables, were introduced in Book 1 of this series. VCe syllables were encountered in Unit 1 of this book. Open syllables are presented for the first time.

Remind students that a bold capital **C** represents a consonant and a bold capital **V** represents a vowel. Then review what students have already learned about syllables.

T: Who can tell me what a syllable is?
S: A syllable is part of a word.
T: Right. What else do you know about a syllable?
S: It has to have a vowel. Also it takes one breath to pronounce it.
T: Good. There are some basic types of syllables in English. We used two of them in Book 1. Let's review those now.

Closed Syllables

Dictate the words on the replica of the student page and have students mark each consonant and each vowel. Students should then be able to fill in the blanks in the description of a closed syllable.

Tell students that the words referred to in Book 1 as one-one-one words are closed syllables. Emphasize that closed syllables must contain a short vowel and end in a consonant. It is the ending consonant that makes the vowel short.

Next, dictate the second set of words and have students write them on the lines provided. Point out that a closed syllable can end in either a single consonant or in a blend or digraph.

Finally, show students several variations of closed syllables, such as:

al, im (beginning with a vowel)
len, cot (**CVC**)
ick, ung (ending with a digraph)
hat, red (one syllable word)

First Syllable	Second Syllable	Whole Word
1. jug	gle	juggle
2. nee	dle	needle
3. lit	tle	little

Look at the second syllable in each word. Each one ends in a consonant plus *le*. Say the second syllable of each of the words above. As you learned in Book 1 of this series, the **Cle** syllable is usually pronounced /Cəl/.

Cle syllables usually come at the _____end_____ of a word.
(beginning *or* end)

Pattern: A **Cle** syllable contains a consonant plus *le* and usually comes at the end of a word.

VCe Syllables. VCe syllables were introduced in Unit 1 of this book. On the lines below, write the words that your teacher dictates.

1. came	3. state	5. save
2. page	4. grade	6. face

What is the final letter in each of these words? ___e___

Does the final letter make a sound? ___no___

What does the final *e* do to the sound of the vowel before the consonant?
_____It makes it long._____

The words you wrote are all **VCe** syllables. They contain a vowel, a consonant, and a silent *e*. The silent *e* makes the vowel long.

Pattern: A **VCe** syllable has a long vowel followed by a consonant and ends in a silent *e*.

36   Lesson 7

Cle Syllables

Dictate the words on the replica of the student page and have students complete the section of the exercise dealing with Cle syllables.

Remind students that Cle syllables are usually pronounced /Cəl/, although sometimes, as in /lit'l/, the schwa is basically silent. Have several students read aloud the Cle syllables of each word you dictated so that they become familiar with the regular pronunciation of this syllable type.

VCe Syllables

Dictate the words on the replica of the student page and have students complete the section of the exercise that deals with VCe syllables. Emphasize that the silent *e* at the end of the syllable makes the vowel long.

Write the patterns below on the board and ask students to pronounce them.

ame	ike	obe	ete
ake	ine	ope	ule

Explain that even though they have not studied most of these patterns, they will be able to pronounce them because they follow the VCe pattern.

Ask students to read the patterns aloud. Then ask them to think of a word that uses each of the patterns above. You may have to help them with *ete* and *ule* because these are less common patterns. (*Complete* and *rule* are words containing these patterns.)

First Syllable	Second Syllable	Whole Word
1. me		me
2. e	ven	even
3. be	ing	being
4. re	cess	recess
5. pre	fix	prefix

The first syllable in each of the words that you wrote is an open syllable. Look at the first syllable in each of the words.

Does the first syllable end in a consonant or a vowel? __a vowel__

Is the vowel long or short? __long__

> **Pattern:** An open syllable ends in a vowel that is usually long.

4 Review of Syllable Types. Write one syllable of each type that you have just learned.

1. Closed __tin__   3. **VCe** __ate__

2. Cle __ple__   4. Open __ra__

5 Writing Sentences. On the lines below, write the sentences that you hear.

1. Is Ray's strength equal to the task?

2. Mrs. Lee complained about the length of the drapes.

3. Dale's knee was especially painful yesterday.

4. Mrs. Baker will move to White Plains in a week or two.

5. She couldn't prove that she hadn't been speeding.

6. The seniors volunteered to do something special for the school.

Lesson 7   37

Open Syllables

Dictate the words on the replica of the student page and have students write them on the lines provided. Explain that open syllables must end in a vowel and that the vowel is usually long. Point out that an open syllable can be just one letter, as in *even* and *open*.

4 Review of Syllable Types

The answers on the replica of the student page are examples. Encourage students to try to think of original examples, rather than copying ones that were used in Exercise 3.

5 Writing Sentences

Instruct students to write the sentences that you dictate, which are on the replica of the student page. Note any specific errors. Design additional sentences, words, or phrases for specific problems.

Patterns found in these sentences include:
—possession (1 and 3)
—adding -*s* or -*es* (2, 4, and 6)
—contractions (5)

Lesson 8
The Word Families *eek*, *eel*, *eet*, and *eem*

Objectives

- **Word Families:** Learn to spell words in the *eek*, *eel*, *eet*, and *eem* families.
- **Sight Words:** Learn to spell *blood*, *flood*, *heart*, *tongue*, *calf*, *half*, *beef*, and *teeth*.
- **Dictionary Skills:** Review alphabetizing by the first three or four letters.
- **Word Building:** Add word families to initial consonants, blends, or digraphs.
- **Syllable Types:** Review the closed, open, VCe, and Cle syllable types. Learn the double vowel syllable type.
- **Creating Sentences:** Write an original paragraph using word family and sight words.
- **Writing Sentences:** Practice writing word family and sight words in context.

Sight Words

Teach the sight words using the methods described on pages 9-12 in the introduction to this book.

Point out the irregular spelling of the short *u* sound in *blood* and *flood*. Ask students to recall some short *u* words from Book 1 that contain the same sound (*bud*, *mud*, *sudden*, etc.). Contrast these spellings with the *oo* in *blood* and *flood*.

Point out the silent *l* in *half* and *calf*. Note that *beef* and *teeth* have the *ee* spelling of the word families in this lesson. Tell students that *f* and *th* are less common endings for *ee* words.

1 Listening

Introduce the words in the *eek* family using the following steps.

1. Say the sound /ēk/ and ask students what letters make the sound.
2. Say the letters e-e-k and ask students what sound they make.
3. Say the word *peek* and ask students what letters spell /ēk/ and what letter spells /p/.
4. Say the word *peek* and ask students what letters spell *peek*.

Follow the same steps to introduce the words in the *eel*, *eet*, and *eem* families.

Point out the *sl* blend in *sleek* and *sleet* and the *sw* blend in *sweet*. Contrast these blends with the digraph *wh* in *wheel*. Point out the silent *k* in *kneel* and the capital *G* in *Greek*. Mention the ending blend in *weekend*. This sound will be covered in Book 3 of this series, but it can be introduced here. Do not worry if students have difficulty with it.

2 Writing Words

Instruct students to write the words that you dictate, which are found on the replica of the student page. Say each word, use it in a phrase or simple sentence, and say the word again. Be sure students capitalize *Greek*.

Lesson 8
The Word Families *eek*, *eel*, *eet*, and *eem*

Sight Words			
blood	heart	calf	beef
flood	tongue	half	teeth

Word Families

eek

eel

eet

eem

1 Listening

Listen to the sound *eek* makes in these words.

| peek | week | cheek | Greek |
| seek | weekend | creek | sleek |

Listen to the sound *eel* makes in these words.

| feel | heel | kneel |
| peel | wheel | steel |

Listen to the sound *eet* makes in these words.

| beet | greet | meeting | fleet |
| feet | sheet | sweet | sleet |

Listen to the sound *eem* makes in these words.

| seem | esteem | redeem |

2 Writing Words. On the lines below, write the words that you hear.

1. feet
2. week
3. heel
4. seeking
5. feel
6. street
7. cheek
8. seem
9. Greek
10. meeting
11. wheel
12. redeem

❸ Dictionary Skills: Alphabetizing. Alphabetize the words in Exercise 2 and write them on the lines below.

1. cheek
2. feet
3. feel
4. Greek
5. heel
6. meeting
7. redeem
8. seeking
9. seem
10. street
11. week
12. wheel

❹ Word Building. Add either *eek, eel, eet,* or *eem* to each of the consonants below to make a word. Do not make the same word twice.

1. b eet
2. f eel
3. f eet
4. m eek
5. p eel
6. s eek
7. s eem
8. w eek
9. cr eek
10. gr eet
11. sh eet
12. sl eet

❺ Reviewing Syllable Types

Closed Syllables. Here are some words with closed syllables. Closed syllables have a short vowel and end with a consonant. Mark the short vowels with the short vowel mark (˘) and write a **C** beside each closed syllable.

1. pĭg C
2. lĭm C ĭt C
3. lăp C
4. trŭm C pĕt C
5. bĕd C
6. năp C kĭn C

A closed syllable has a __short__ vowel and ends with a __consonant.__

Open Syllables. Here are some words with open syllables. Open syllables usually end with a long vowel. Mark the long vowels with a long vowel mark (¯) and write an **O** beside each open syllable.

1. shē O
2. ē O gō O
3. gō O
4. bē O twēen
5. mē O
6. rē O dēem

An open syllable usually ends with a __long__ vowel.

Lesson 8   39

❸ Dictionary Skills: Alphabetizing

This exercise requires students to alphabetize words by the first two, three, and four letters. You may want to develop additional reinforcement activities for any students who are still having difficulty alphabetizing words. For ideas, see pages 7-8 in the introduction to Book 1 Teacher's Edition.

❹ Word Building

Have students add one of the word families to each consonant, blend, or digraph to make a word. Encourage them to use all of the word families at least once. The answers given on the replica of the student page are examples. Accept all correctly spelled words.

❺ Reviewing Syllable Types

This exercise reviews the four syllable types covered in Lesson 7. Review the short and long vowel markings before students begin the exercise. Remind them also that recognizing syllable types will help them to pronounce and spell words correctly.

Dictionaries may show a short *i* sound for the first vowel in *between*, /bĭ twēn/. However, /bē twēn/ is also a correct pronunciation. For the purposes of this exercise, accept either a long or short vowel mark for the first syllable. If students do use the short vowel mark, explain that sometimes an open syllable has a short vowel sound rather than a long vowel sound, particularly when the open syllable is unaccented.

Cle Syllables. Here are some words with **Cle** syllables. These syllables contain a consonant plus *le*. Write **Cle** beside each syllable of this type.

1. bun   dle Cle   3. peo   ple Cle   5. nee   dle Cle

2. lit   tle Cle   4. crum   ble Cle   6. bub   ble Cle

A **Cle** syllable contains a consonant plus ___le___.

VCe Syllables. Here are some words with **VCe** syllables. **VCe** syllables have a long vowel followed by a consonant and a silent *e*. Mark the long vowels with a long vowel mark ($^-$), and write **VCe** beside each syllable of this type.

1. bāke VCe   3. pāle VCe   5. dāte VCe

2. mis   plāce VCe   4. pāve VCe ment   6. bāse VCe ball

A **VCe** syllable has a ___long___ vowel, a consonant, and a ___silent___ *e* at the end of it.

6 **Double Vowel Syllables.** Sometimes two vowels that come together make one sound. For example, two *e*'s together make a long *e* sound. *A* and *i* together make a long *a* sound. Syllables in which two vowels together make one vowel sound are called double vowel syllables.

Here are some words with double vowel syllables. Write **D** beside each syllable which has a double vowel.

1. paid D   3. beef D   5. ex   plain D

2. re   deem D   4. main D tain D   6. vol   un   teer D

Pattern: A double vowel syllable has two vowels together that make one sound.

6 Double Vowel Syllables

This exercise introduces a fifth syllable type, double vowel syllables. Point out to students that double vowel syllables often have a long vowel sound.

All of the double vowel syllables in this exercise end with a consonant to avoid confusion. Double vowel syllables that do not end with a consonant can be confused with open syllables. For instance, *free* is a double vowel syllable that sounds like an open syllable. If the vowel sound is spelled with two vowels, then it is a double vowel syllable.

7 **Creating Sentences.** On a separate sheet of paper, write a paragraph describing this picture. Think about what is happening in the picture and what may happen soon. Use some of the following long *e* words in your sentences.

committee	three	coffee	seem	agree
meeting	senior	sweet rolls	being	cheer
greet	volunteers	needle	beyond	react

Retired Senior Volunteer Project

8 **Writing Sentences.** On the lines below, write the sentences that you hear.

1. Mrs. Peel will buy half of the beef.
2. Three volunteers gave blood last weekend.
3. Lee seems to feel the calf is doing well.
4. Mr. Weeks had to have three teeth filled.
5. Mrs. Meeker bit her tongue when she tripped.
6. Dave sang "Let Me Call You Sweetheart."
7. This week's meeting will be short and sweet.
8. If it keeps on raining, the creek may flood.

Lesson 8   41

---

7 Creating Sentences

Discuss the illustration with students before they begin to write. Encourage them to use as many long *e* and sight words as they can.

If students ask how to spell a word that they have not studied, encourage them to look it up in the dictionary. Remember that errors in words that haven't been studied shouldn't be treated negatively. Point out any parts of the word that are spelled correctly and praise the effort.

8 Writing Sentences

Instruct students to write the sentences that you dictate, which are on the replica of the student page. Note any specific errors. Design additional sentences, words, or phrases for specific problems.

Sentence number 6 contains a song title. You may want to review capitalization and punctuation of titles, or you may choose not to hold students responsible for these elements. You may also want to review Doubling Pattern 1 from Book 1 before beginning this dictation.

Patterns found in these sentences include:
—adding *-s* or *-es* (2, 3, and 8)
—irregular verb forms (2)
—Doubling Pattern 1 (5)
—possession (7)

Lesson 9

The Word Families *een*, *eed*, *eep*, and *eech*

Objectives

- **Word Families:** Learn to spell words in the *een*, *eed*, *eep*, and *eech* families.
- **Sight Words:** Learn to spell *rough*, *tough*, *enough*, *dough*, *though*, and *although*.
  Use the sight words to complete sentences.
- **Pattern:** Learn to form numbers with *teen*.
- **Syllable Types:** Review the five syllable types previously introduced.
- **Writing by Syllables:** Write dictated words by syllables, noting syllable types.
- **Creating Sentences:** Use designated words in original sentences.
- **Dictionary Skills:** Look up the principal parts of specific irregular verbs.
  Use irregular verb forms to complete sentences.
- **Writing Sentences:** Practice writing word family and sight words in context.

Sight Words

Teach the sight words using the methods described on pages 9-12 in the introduction to this book.

These sight words should be taught in groups of three, stressing the /ŭf/ pronunciation of *ough* in *rough*, *tough*, and *enough*, and the /ō/ pronunciation of *ough* in *dough*, *though*, and *although*. Point out that *although* is the word *though* with a prefix added.

Lesson 9
The Word Families *een*, *eed*, *eep*, and *eech*

Sight Words	
rough	dough
tough	though
enough	although

Word Families	
een	
eed	
eep	
eech	

❶ Listening

een — Listen to the sound *een* makes in these words.

seen	teen	thirteen	keen
green	teenager	fourteen	screen
queen	between	fifteen	canteen

eed — Listen to the sound *eed* makes in these words.

feed	weed	speed	bleed
need	deed	succeed	greed
seed	indeed	proceed	agreed

eep — Listen to the sound *eep* makes in these words.

sheep	deep	jeep	weep
sleep	keep	peep	sweep
asleep	doorkeeper	creep	steep

eech — Listen to the sound *eech* makes in these words.

speech	speechless	screech

❷ Writing Words. On the lines below, write the words that you hear.

1. need
2. sleep
3. fourteen
4. indeed
5. seen
6. beeper
7. speech
8. proceed
9. between

42   Lesson 9

---

❶ Listening

Introduce the words in the *een* family using the following steps.

1. Say the sound /ēn/ and ask students what letters make the sound.
2. Say the letters *e-e-n* and ask students what sound they make.
3. Say the word *seen* and ask students what letters spell /ēn/ and what letter spells /s/.
4. Say the word *seen* and ask students what letters spell *seen*.

Follow the same steps to introduce the words in the *eed*, *eep*, and *eech* families.

Point out the *bl* blend in *bleed* and the *cr* blend in *creep*. Note that the *cr* is also present in the *scr* blend found in *screen* and *screech*. Don't worry if students have trouble with this blend. It will be dealt with more thoroughly in Book 3 of this series.

❷ Writing Words

Instruct students to write the words that you dictate, which are found on the replica of the student page. Say each word, use it in a phrase or simple sentence, and say the word again.

3 **Using Sight Words.** Write one of the sight words from this lesson in each blank in the sentences below.

1. My cat's tongue is so ___rough___ it feels like sandpaper.

2. Before Jane could bake the bread, she had to let the ___dough___ rise.

3. Slow cooking in a spicy sauce can make ___tough___ meat more tender.

4. It was warm and sunny all day, even ___though___ the weatherman predicted rain.

5. ___Although___ some unexpected guests came to the party, there was ___enough___ food to go around.

4 **Forming Numbers with *Teen*.** Write the words that your teacher dictates.

1. _thirteen_   4. _sixteen_   6. _eighteen_

2. _fourteen_   5. _seventeen_   7. _nineteen_

3. _fifteen_

What pattern is present in all of these words? ____teen____

Pattern: *Teen* is used to make the numbers thirteen through nineteen.

5 **Reviewing Syllable Types.** The five types of syllables you have studied so far are listed below. An example of each type is given. Write another example of each type of syllable on the lines provided.

Syllable Type	Example	Your Example
1. Closed	set	sell
2. Open	re	de
3. Cle	ble	ple
4. VCe	ake	ade
5. Double Vowel	eem	aid

3 **Using Sight Words**

This exercise provides practice in using and seeing the sight words in context.

4 **Forming Numbers with *Teen***

Point out that all these words except *thirteen*, *fifteen*, and *eighteen* are formed regularly, i.e., the suffix *teen* is added to the number word. *Three* and *five* are changed to form *thirteen* and *fifteen*, and the final *t* is dropped from *eight* when *teen* is added.

5 **Reviewing Syllable Types**

The answers given on the replica of the student page are examples. Accept all correct responses.

6 **Writing Words by Syllables.** Write the words your teacher dictates by syllables. Then write the whole word. Beside each syllable write the syllable type (C for closed, O for open, Cle, VCe, or D for double vowel).

First Syllable	Second Syllable	Third Syllable	Whole Word
1. fif C	teen D		fifteen
2. pro O	ceed D		proceed
3. pud C	dle Cle		puddle
4. ro O	bot C		robot
5. es C	cape VCe		escape
6. Hal C	lo O	ween D	Halloween
7. fas C	cin C	ate VCe	fascinate
8. fan C	tas C	tic C	fantastic

Challenge word:

e O   ven C   tu O   al C   ly O   eventually

7 **Creating Sentences.** Use a form of each of the words below in a sentence. Look up their definitions in a dictionary if necessary.

1. proceed _____

_____

2. fascinate _____

_____

3. fantastic _____

_____

---

6 **Writing Words by Syllables**

This exercise is best done with your close supervision. Review the various syllable types before you begin the exercise. Dictate the words by syllables, emphasizing the syllables and having students write them on the lines provided. Point out that the number of blanks for each word indicates the number of syllables in that particular word.

When all the words have been dictated, have students identify each syllable by type. You may want to do the first two or three together as a group using the following approach.

T: Listen to the word *fifteen*. How many syllables does it have?
S: Two.
T: Good. What is the first syllable?
S: *Fif.*
T: Right. What type of syllable is *fif*?
S: Closed.
T: Right. How do you know?
S: It has a short vowel and ends in a consonant.
T: We know that a closed syllable has a short vowel. The sound /ĭ/ is represented by what vowel?

S: *I.*
T: Good. How do we spell *fif*?
S: *F-i-f.*
T: Good. Write a *C* after *fif* in your books. What is the second syllable in *fifteen*?
S: *Teen.*
T: Right. What kind of syllable is it?
S: A double vowel syllable.
T: Excellent. What is the double vowel?
S: *E-e.*
T: Good. How do we spell *teen*?
S: *T-e-e-n.*
T: Good. Write a *D* after *teen* in your books.

Help students as needed. Don't worry about conventional division of syllables. If you feel students need the extra practice, have them mark the vowels with the long (-) or short (˘) vowel marks.

7 **Creating Sentences**

This exercise gives students the opportunity to use three of the words in Exercise 6 in original sentences. If your students need this kind of activity, you might have them use all of the words in sentences.

8 **Dictionary Skills: Irregular Verbs.** Look up the following irregular verbs in the dictionary, and write the different forms in the appropriate columns.

Present Tense	Past Tense	*Have, Has,* or *Had* + Verb	*-ing* Form of Verb
1. see	saw	seen	seeing
2. feed	fed	fed	feeding
3. sleep	slept	slept	sleeping
4. feel	felt	felt	feeling
5. keep	kept	kept	keeping

9 **Using Irregular Verbs.** Fill in the blanks in these sentences with the correct form of the verb in parentheses.

1. (feed) Have the dog and cat been _____fed_____?

2. (see) Have you _____seen_____ my notebook anywhere?

3. (feel) Dean _____felt_____ good about the job he had done.

4. (sleep) Last night the baby _____slept_____ all through the night.

5. (keep) Jean _____kept_____ practicing until she had learned how to type.

10 **Writing Sentences.** On the lines below, write the sentences that you hear.

1. This cut of beef is very tough.
2. The kids eventually fell asleep.
3. Was there enough cake to feed everyone?
4. Have you seen Doreen's new green jeep?
5. Her three sons are between fifteen and eighteen.
6. Mr. Weeks gave a very long speech at the meeting.

8 **Dictionary Skills: Irregular Verbs**

Review the principal parts of verbs before students begin this exercise. If students are keeping a table of irregular verbs in their notebooks, have them add these when they finish the exercise.

9 **Using Irregular Verbs**

This exercise gives students the opportunity to use irregular verb forms in context.

10 **Writing Sentences**

Instruct students to write the sentences that you dictate, which are on the replica of the student page. Note any specific errors. Design additional sentences, words, or phrases for specific problems.

Patterns found in these sentences include:
—polysyllabic words (2)
—adding *-s* or *-es* (2 and 5)
—irregular verb forms (4 and 6)
—possession (4)
—forming numbers with *teen* (5)

Lesson 10

The Word Families *ea*, *ead*, *eak*, and *eam*

Objectives

- **Word Families:** Learn to spell words in the *ea*, *ead*, *eak*, and *eam* families.
- **Sight Words:** Learn to spell *oh*, *owe*, *coarse*, *course*, *double*, and *trouble*.
- **Homonyms:** Learn to use correctly *oh/owe* and *coarse/course*. Learn that the digraphs *ee* and *ea* produce many homonym pairs.
- **Creating Sentences:** Use homonyms in original sentences.
- **Dictionary Skills:** Practice using guide words to find words in the dictionary. Distinguish between homonym pairs spelled *ee* and *ea*.
- **Word Building:** Fill in *ee* or *ea* to spell the correct word in context.
- **Writing by Syllables:** Write dictated words by syllables.
- **Writing Sentences:** Practice writing word family and sight words in context.

Sight Words

Teach the sight words using the methods described on pages 9-12 in the introduction to this book.

Point out the two pairs of homonyms in these sight words: *oh/owe* and *coarse/course*. Note also that *double* and *trouble* end in Cle syllables.

❶ Listening

Introduce the words in the *ea* family using the following steps.

1. Say the sound /ē/ and ask students what letters make the sound in the first group of words.
2. Say the letters *e-a* and ask students what sound they make.
3. Say the word *sea* and ask students what letters spell /ē/ and what letter spells /s/.

4. Say the word *sea* and ask students what letters spell *sea*.

Follow the same steps to introduce the words in the *ead*, *eak*, and *eam* families.

Point out the schwa sound in *season* and *reason*. Ask students to make a mental picture of the spelling of these two words paying special attention to the *o-n* at the end.

Point out the *sn* blend in *sneakers* and the *dr* blend in *dream*. Be sure students can hear both sounds in each blend.

Point out that *read* and *lead* have

alternate pronunciations: /rĕd/ and /lĕd/.

Tell students that *e-a* is another way to spell long *e*. Point out that they have learned three ways to spell long *e* so far: *e* in an open syllable, *ee*, and *ea*. Ask students to give you some words for each spelling of long *e*.

❷ Writing Words

Instruct students to write the words that you dictate, which are found on the replica of the student page. Say each word, use it in a phrase or simple sentence, and say the word again.

Lesson 10

The Word Families *ea*, *ead*, *eak*, and *eam*

Sight Words		
oh	coarse	double
owe	course	trouble

Word Families

ea

❶ Listening

Listen to the sound *ea* makes in these words.

sea	tea	pea	eager
season	teaspoon	plea	measles
reason			

ead

Listen to the sound *ead* makes in these words.

bead	plead	read	lead

eak

Listen to the sound *eak* makes in these words.

peak	leak	squeak	creak
speak	weak	streak	sneakers

eam

Listen to the sound *eam* makes in these words.

cream	team	beam	seam
scream	steam	dream	stream

❷ Writing Words. On the lines below, write the words that you hear.

1. lead
2. weak
3. eager
4. dreamer
5. speak
6. read
7. cream
8. seasoning
9. steaming

46   Lesson 10

3 Homonyms: *Oh/Owe* and *Coarse/Course*. Read the following sentences and notice how the homonyms are used.

1. *Oh*, how I wish I could finish this job!
2. We *owe* only one more payment on the furniture.

3. This cloth has a *coarse* texture.
4. Steve is taking a *course* at the community college.

Now write one sentence of your own for each of these words.

oh _____

owe _____

coarse _____

course _____

4 Dictionary Skills: Guide Words. Below are pairs of guide words that might be found on dictionary pages. Decide if the words listed below them would appear on the dictionary page that has those guide words. Underline each word that would be found on that page.

1. **flashcube — fledgling**
   <u>flea</u>   flew   flee   feel

2. **pediment — pencil**
   <u>peek</u>   peal   <u>peel</u>   peak

3. **reduce — reflex**
   read   <u>reek</u>   <u>reed</u>   <u>reel</u>

4. **scuffle — seamy**
   <u>seal</u>   seen   screen   seem

5. **teak — Teflon**
   tea   <u>tee</u>   <u>team</u>   <u>teem</u>

6. **we — weave**
   <u>weak</u>   <u>weary</u>   week   weep

Lesson 10   47

3 Homonyms: *Oh/Owe* and *Coarse/Course*

This exercise provides an opportunity for students to use these two pairs of homonyms in original sentences. If they have difficulty with *coarse* and *course*, provide additional sample sentences or have them look up the definitions in the dictionary.

4 Dictionary Skills: Guide Words

Remind students that the guide words at the top of a dictionary page are the first and last entry words on that page. Do the first one or two items in this exercise as a group.

One technique for teaching the use of guide words is to have students cross out, cover up, or otherwise eliminate common letters in the entry word and the guide words and then determine if the remaining letter(s) fit between the guide words. Write *flashcube, fledgling,* and *flea* on the board.

T: *Flashcube, fledgling,* and *flea* all begin with the same two letters. (Draw a line through the *f* and the *l* in each word.) What is the third letter in *flea*?
S: *E.*
T: Right. What is the third letter in *flashcube*?
S: It's an *a.*
T: Does the *e* in *flea* come after the *a* in *flashcube*?
S: Yes.
T: Then *flea* will come after *flashcube.* So now we know that *flea* will be found on this page if it comes before *fledgling.*
Look at *fledgling.* Is the third letter in *fledgling* an *e*?
S: Yes.
T: Since *e* is the third letter in both words, we need to look at the fourth letter. What is the fourth letter in *flea*?
S: *A.*
T: What is the fourth letter in *fledgling*?
S: *D.*
T: Does *a* come before *d*?
S: Yes.
T: Then *flea* comes after *flashcube* and before *fledgling.* Will *flea* be found on this dictionary page?
S: Yes.

Follow the same procedure for *flew, flee,* and *feel.*

5 Dictionary Skills: Homonyms. The long *e* can be spelled many ways. Two spellings of long *e* are *ee* and *ea*. There are many homonym pairs, such as *sea* and *see*, which use both spellings. The correct spelling depends upon the meaning of the word in context. A dictionary can help you choose the correct word from a pair of homonyms. Answer the following questions using a dictionary when you need to.

1. When people run away, do they *flea* or *flee*?   flee

2. Is the shore by the *sea* or the *see*?   sea

3. Are there seven days in a *weak* or a *week*?   week

4. Is a quick look a *peak* or a *peek*?   peek

5. Does a jacket have *seams* or *seems*?   seams

6. When it rains very hard, is it *teaming* or *teeming*?   teeming

7. Is a plant that grows in a marsh a *read* or a *reed*?   reed

8. For a soothing drink, would you pour a cup of *tea* or *tee*?   tea

6 Word Building. Write either *ee* or *ea* in the blanks in the sentences below. The letters you choose will depend on the meaning of the word in the context of the sentence.

1. Jane felt w_e__a_k after her operation.

2. Gail hopes her t_e__a_m will win the game.

3. I s_e__e_ a fl_e__a_ on your cat.

4. To begin a game of golf, you must t_e__e_ off.

5. The child p_e__e_ked around the corner but wouldn't come in.

6. Can you repair the s_e__a_m in my jeans?

7. The back yard is t_e__e_ming with insects.

8. I s_e__e_m to remember reading something about that.

9. Gene's children asked him to r_e__a_d a story to them.

10. The mountain climbers had nearly reached the p_e__a_k when night fell.

5 Dictionary Skills: Homonyms

Students will already be familiar with many of these words, so they won't have to look up their definitions. Encourage students to use guide words to help them find the homonyms that they do look up.

6 Word Building

The emphasis in this exercise is on discriminating between the *ee* and *ea* spellings in these homonym pairs. Remind students that the correct spelling depends upon the meaning of the word in context.

Note students who have particular difficulty with homonyms. Determine if they also have difficulty learning sight words. If so, review the strategies for learning sight words in the introduction to this book. These strategies can also be used with homonyms.

7 **Writing Words by Syllables.** Write the words that you hear one syllable at a time. Then write the whole word on the line at the right. Use the syllable type to help you spell the word.

First Syllable	Second Syllable	Third Syllable	Whole Word
1. lo	cate		locate
2. gen	tle		gentle
3. rea	son		reason
4. fe	male		female
5. stag	nate		stagnate
6. pi	o	neer	pioneer
7. con	fis	cate	confiscate
8. sev	en	teen	seventeen

Challenge word:

mon	o	nu	cle	o	sis	mononucleosis

8 **Writing Sentences.** On the lines below, write the sentences that you hear.

1. Do you take cream in your coffee?
2. My shoes squeak, so I'll put on my sneakers.
3. Mrs. Beecher owes seventeen cents on that letter.
4. Some people call the Greer twins "double trouble."
5. Did Kathleen give any reason for not being on the team?
6. Did you read about Mr. Meeker's speech?
7. Of course he would prefer to speak to all of us at once.
8. I dreamed that I had the measles and mononucleosis, too.

Lesson 10   49

7 Writing Words by Syllables

Remind students that the number of blanks indicates the number of syllables in the word. Dictate each word by syllables, emphasizing the syllables. Then pronounce the whole word normally.

If students have difficulty spelling two- and three-syllable words, tell them to concentrate on the types of syllables they hear in the words. Encourage them to pronounce the words syllable by syllable. For students who continue to have difficulty, pronounce the words by syllables, encouraging them to spell each syllable after you say it.

Additional Activities:

Have students identify the types of syllables they have written by using C for closed, O for open, **VCe**, **Cle**, or D for double vowel syllables.

Have students look up the meanings of any of these words that they don't already know.

Have them use some of the words in original sentences.

8 Writing Sentences

Instruct students to write the sentences that you dictate, which are on the replica of the student page. Note any specific errors. Design additional sentences, words, or phrases for specific problems.

Sentence 5 contains the name *Kathleen*, which can be spelled with a *K* or a *C*. Generally speaking, a phonetically correct spelling for the proper names in these exercises should be acceptable.

Patterns found in these sentences include:
—contractions (2)
—homonyms (3, 5, 6, and 7)
—adding -*s* or -*es* (2, 3, and 4)
—forming numbers with -*teen* (3)
—possession (6)
—polysyllabic words (8)

Lesson 11
The Word Families *eat*, *eal*, *ean*, and *eap*

Objectives

- **Word Families:** Learn to spell words in the *eat*, *eal*, *ean*, and *eap* families.
- **Sight Words:** Learn to spell *busy*, *bury*, *color*, *sugar*, *purpose*, *suppose*, *else*, and *wolf*.
- **Dictionary Skills:** Distinguish between homonym pairs spelled with the *ee* and *ea* digraphs.
- **Word Building:** Fill in *ee* or *ea* to spell the correct word in context.
- **Syllable Types:** Review five types of syllables by categorizing examples.
- **Writing by Syllables:** Write dictated words by syllables.
- **Creating Sentences:** Write an original paragraph using word family and sight words.
- **Writing Sentences:** Practice writing word family and sight words in context.

Sight Words

Teach the sight words using the methods described on pages 9-12 in the introduction to this book.

Draw attention to some of the unusual features of these words, such as the /ĭz/ in *busy*, the /ĕr/ in *bury*, the /sh/ in *sugar*, and the pronunciation of *pose* in *purpose* as /pŭs/. Ask students for a homonym for *bury*. (They should remember *berry*, a sight word in Lesson 6.)

Lesson 11
The Word Families *eat*, *eal*, *ean*, and *eap*

Sight Words			
busy	color	purpose	else
bury	sugar	suppose	wolf

Word Families

eat

1 Listening

Listen to the sound *eat* makes in these words.

eat	heat	neat	cheat
beat	heater	seat	treat
meat	wheat	repeat	defeat

eal

Listen to the sound *eal* makes in these words.

meal	deal	appeal
real	heal	reveal
seal	steal	conceal

ean

Listen to the sound *ean* makes in these words.

bean	Jean	lean
dean	mean	clean

eap

Listen to the sound *eap* makes in these words.

heap	leap	cheap

2 Writing Words. On the lines below, write the words that you hear.

1. seat
2. bean
3. reap
4. meat
5. real
6. cheaper
7. meaning
8. repeated
9. reveal

---

1 Listening

Introduce the words in the *eat* family using the following steps.

1. Say the sound /ēt/ and ask students what letters make the sound.
2. Say the letters e-a-t and ask students what sound they make.
3. Say the word *beat* and ask students what letters spell /ēt/ and what letter spells /b/.
4. Say the word *beat* and ask students what letters spell *beat*.

Follow the same steps to introduce the words in the *eal*, *ean*, and *eap* families.

Remind students that these words all contain double vowels.

2 Writing Words

Instruct students to write the words that you dictate, which are found on the replica of the student page. Say each word, use it in a phrase or simple sentence, and say the word again.

3 **Dictionary Skills: Homonyms.** Below are several more sets of homonyms spelled with *ea* and *ee*. Answer the following questions, using a dictionary to help you select the correct spelling based on the context.

1. Do bells *peal* or *peel*?   _____peal_____
2. Is a dark red vegetable a *beat* or a *beet*?   _____beet_____
3. Will a cut on your finger *heal* or *heel*?   _____heal_____
4. Did the thief *steal* or *steel*?   _____steal_____
5. Will you *meat* or *meet* your friend for lunch?   _____meet_____
6. Is a remarkable achievement a *feat* or a *feet*?   _____feat_____
7. Do baby chicks *cheap* or *cheep*?   _____cheep_____
8. Does a fishing rod have a *real* or a *reel*?   _____reel_____

4 **Word Building.** Write either *ee* or *ea* in the blanks in the sentences below. The letters you choose will depend on the meaning of the word.

1. The Buffalo Bills b_e_ _a_t the Pittsburgh Steelers.
2. Did the thief st_e_ _a_l anything when he broke into your car?
3. Those peaches will be ch_e_ _a_per to buy in a few weeks.
4. The h_e_ _e_l of Grace's shoe broke off when she tripped.
5. Steve is a vegetarian, so he never eats m_e_ _a_t.
6. Mrs. Blair's f_e_ _e_t hurt from so much walking.
7. Jane's dream seemed so r_e_ _a_l that it frightened her.
8. Jean has a new set of stainless st_e_ _e_l pots and pans.
9. Gary was p_e_ _e_ling potatoes in the kitchen when we arrived.
10. Finishing the marathon was a remarkable f_e_ _a_t for Lee.

3 Dictionary Skills: Homonyms

Students will already be familiar with many of these words, so they won't have to look up their definitions. Encourage students to use guide words to help them find the homonyms that they do look up.

4 Word Building

The emphasis in this exercise is on discriminating between the *ee* and *ea* spellings in these homonym pairs. Remind students that the correct spelling depends upon the meaning of the word in context.

Note students who are still having difficulty with homonyms. Review the strategies for learning sight words in the introduction to this book. These strategies can also be used with homonyms.

5 **Reviewing Syllable Types.** Write each syllable below on a line under the correct heading. The first one has been done to get you started.

✓neer	dle	ro	pip	ble
sep	tic	ne	a	pane
rain	sipe	ple	tane	ceed

Closed
1. _____sep_____
2. _____tic_____
3. _____pip_____

Open
1. _____ro_____
2. _____ne_____
3. _____a_____

Cle
1. _____dle_____
2. _____ple_____
3. _____ble_____

VCe
1. _____sipe_____
2. _____tane_____
3. _____pane_____

Double
1. _____neer_____
2. _____rain_____
3. _____ceed_____

6 **Writing Words by Syllables.** Write the words that your teacher dictates one syllable at a time. Then write the whole word.

	First Syllable	Second Syllable	Third Syllable	Whole Word
1.	ad	dress		address
2.	do	nate		donate
3.	re	heat		reheat
4.	ca	ble		cable
5.	pre	tend		pretend
6.	de	pos	it	deposit
7.	es	tab	lish	establish
8.	le	gal	ize	legalize

52   Lesson 11

5 **Reviewing Syllable Types**

This exercise reviews the five syllable types presented in this text. Review the attributes of each syllable type before the students begin. Be sure they understand that they are to categorize the syllables by writing them on the lines under the appropriate headings.

6 **Writing Words by Syllables**

Dictate each word by syllables, emphasizing the syllables. Then pronounce the whole word normally. Remind students that the number of blanks indicates the number of syllables in the word. If students have difficulty with any of these words, help them to isolate the problem syllable and listen to it.

Don't worry about formal syllable divisions. Emphasize the division students hear.

Additional Activities:

Have students identify the types of syllables they have written.

Have them look up the meanings of any of the words that they don't already know.

Have them use some of the words in original sentences.

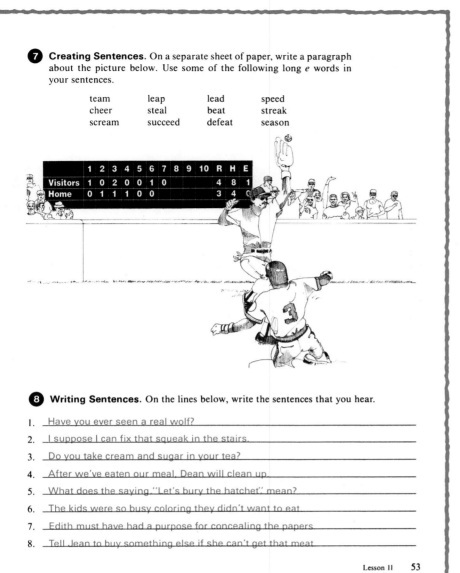

7 Creating Sentences. On a separate sheet of paper, write a paragraph about the picture below. Use some of the following long *e* words in your sentences.

team	leap	lead	speed
cheer	steal	beat	streak
scream	succeed	defeat	season

	1	2	3	4	5	6	7	8	9	10	R	H	E
Visitors	1	0	2	0	0	1	0				4	8	1
Home	0	1	1	1	0	0					3	4	

8 Writing Sentences. On the lines below, write the sentences that you hear.

1. Have you ever seen a real wolf?
2. I suppose I can fix that squeak in the stairs.
3. Do you take cream and sugar in your tea?
4. After we've eaten our meal, Dean will clean up.
5. What does the saying, "Let's bury the hatchet," mean?
6. The kids were so busy coloring they didn't want to eat.
7. Edith must have had a purpose for concealing the papers.
8. Tell Jean to buy something else if she can't get that meat.

Lesson 11   53

7 Creating Sentences

Discuss the illustration with students before they begin to write. Encourage them to use as many long *e* and sight words as they can.

If students ask how to spell a word that they have not studied, encourage them to look it up in the dictionary. Remember that errors in words that haven't been studied shouldn't be treated negatively. Point out any parts of the word that are spelled correctly and praise the effort.

8 Writing Sentences

Instruct students to write the sentences that you dictate, which are on the replica of the student page. Note any specific errors. Design additional sentences, words, or phrases for specific problems.

Patterns found in these sentences include:
—homonyms (1, 2, 3, 5, and 8)
—irregular verb forms (1 and 4)
—contractions (4, 5, 6, and 8)
—adding *-s* or *-es* (6 and 7)

Lesson 12

The Word Families *each*, *east*, and *ear*

Objectives

- **Word Families:** Learn to spell words in the *each*, *east*, and *ear* families.
- **Sight Words:** Learn to spell *been*, *many*, *broad*, *machine*, *clothes*, *material*, *leaf*, and *leash*.
- **Pattern:** Discover that if the first syllable of a two-syllable word is closed, the second syllable usually begins with a consonant. When the two middle consonants are the same, only one will be heard.
- **Syllable Types:** Review five types of syllables by categorizing examples.
- **Writing by Syllables:** Write dictated words by syllables.
- **Homonyms:** Learn to discriminate between *hear* and *here*.
- **Creating Sentences:** Use homonyms in original sentences.
- **Writing Sentences:** Practice writing word family and sight words in context.

Sight Words

Teach the sight words using the methods described on pages 9-12 in the introduction to this book. Note the short vowel sound for the *ee* spelling in *been*. Point out the /sh/ pronunciation of *ch* in *machine* and the silent *th* in *clothes*. Note that *leaf* and *leash* have the *ea* spelling for long *e*, but that *f* and *sh* are less common endings for *ea* words.

❶ Listening

Introduce the words in the *each* family using the following steps.

1. Say the sound /ēch/ and ask students what letters make the sound.

2. Say the letters *e-a-c-h* and ask students what sound they make.
3. Say the word *teach* and ask students what letters spell /ēch/ and what letter spells /t/.
4. Say the word *teach* and ask students what letters spell *teach*.

Follow the same steps to introduce the words in the *east* and *ear* families.

Pay careful attention to the *east* family. The ending blend may be difficult for some students. Draw attention to the *st* by pronouncing it carefully and asking students to pronounce it carefully. Do not separate it from the *ea*.

As with *eer*, many dictionaries will not show *ear* family words as having long *e* sounds. However, *ear* is included here because the sound is very close to the long *e* sound.

❷ Writing Words

Instruct students to write the words that you dictate, which are found on the replica of the student page. Say each word, use it in a phrase or simple sentence, and say the word again.

Lesson 12

The Word Families *each*, *east*, and *ear*

Sight Words			
been	broad	clothes	leaf
many	machine	material	leash

Word Families

each

east

ear

❶ Listening

Listen to the sound that *each* makes in these words.

each	beach	peach	reach
teach	bleach	impeach	preach
teacher	unbleached	impeachment	

Listen to the sound that *east* makes in these words.

east	beast	feast	least

Listen to the sound that *ear* makes in these words.

ear	hear	year	weary
dear	near	clear	appear
fear	rear	shears	disappear

❷ Writing Words. On the lines below, write the words that you hear.

1. dear
2. least
3. beach
4. clear
5. teaching
6. near
7. reach
8. fearless
9. impeach
10. feasting
11. bleached
12. appeared

❸ Finding a Pattern

Part A. Write the words that you hear one syllable at a time. Then answer the questions below.

1. con   ceal
2. in   deed
3. ad   mit

4. por   tray
5. im   peach
6. com   plain

Look at the first syllable of each word you wrote. What type of syllable is the first syllable?

closed

Look at the second syllable of each word you wrote. Does the second syllable begin with a consonant or a vowel?   consonant

> **Pattern:** If the first syllable of a two-syllable word is closed, the second syllable usually begins with a consonant.

Part B. When the first syllable ends with the same consonant that the second syllable begins with, you will hear only one consonant sound in the middle of the word. If you do not hear two consonant sounds, the middle consonant is usually doubled.

Examples: muffin   tennis   sudden

Write the words that you hear one syllable at a time. Then answer the questions below.

1. kit   ten
2. gos   sip

3. pup   pet
4. rib   bon

Do the words you wrote follow the pattern in Part A?   yes

Look at the last letter in each first syllable and the first letter in each second syllable. What do you notice about these letters?   They are the same.

> **Pattern:** If the first syllable of a two-syllable word is closed, the second syllable usually begins with a consonant. If you do not hear two consonant sounds, the middle consonant is usually doubled.

Lesson 12   55

❸ Finding a Pattern

This exercise draws attention to the fact that in words of more than one syllable, if the first syllable is closed, the second syllable will usually begin with a consonant. In other words, there will be two consonants in the middle of the word. When these two consonants are the same, students will only hear one consonant and may tend to omit one when spelling the word.

When students have completed Part B, draw attention to the the use of the schwa in *ribbon*. Point out that *on* as an ending sometimes is pronounced with a schwa. Ask them if they remember any other words that end in *on* and are pronounced with a schwa (*season* and *reason* were family words in Lesson 10).

4 **Reviewing Syllable Types.** Write each syllable below on a line under the correct heading.

ceal	cle	re	nit	tle
sis	son	be	o	pone
site	tain	kle	tine	deed

Closed

1. _sis_
2. _son_
3. _nit_

Open

1. _re_
2. _be_
3. _o_

Cle

1. _cle_
2. _kle_
3. _tle_

VCe

1. _site_
2. _tine_
3. _pone_

Double

1. _ceal_
2. _tain_
3. _deed_

5 **Writing Words by Syllables.** Write the words that your teacher dictates one syllable at a time. Then write the whole word. Use the syllable types to help you spell the word.

First Syllable	Second Syllable	Third Syllable	Whole Word
1. mid	dle		middle
2. dic	tate		dictate
3. grap	ple		grapple
4. com	pen	sate	compensate
5. mag	net	ic	magnetic
6. re	ig	nite	reignite

Challenge word:

re	ap	pear	ing	reappearing

4 **Reviewing Syllable Types**

Review the attributes of the five syllable types before students begin this exercise.

Additional Activity:

Have students select one syllable of each type and add one or more syllables to make a word.

5 **Writing Words by Syllables**

Dictate each word by syllables, emphasizing the syllables. Then pronounce the whole word normally. Remind students that the number of blanks indicates the number of syllables in the word.

Additional Activities:

Have students identify the types of syllables they have written by using C for closed, O for open, **VCe**, **Cle**, or D for double vowel syllables.

Have students look up the meanings of any of these words that they don't already know.

Have them use some of the words in original sentences.

Have students tell you what *ignite* means. Let them use the dictionary if necessary. Review *re-* as a prefix meaning *again*.

6 **Homonyms:** *Hear* and *Here*. Read the following sentences and notice how the homonyms are used.

1. We *hear* with our ears.
2. I can't *hear* what you are saying.
3. *Here* comes my sister now.
4. Bring those boxes over *here*.

In the sentences below, fill in either *hear* or *here*.

1. If you will wait _____ here _____, I will be right back.
2. I _____ hear _____ that James is going to come home.
3. Did you _____ hear _____ the telephone ring?
4. The wind scattered the leaves _____ here _____ and there.

Now write one sentence of your own for each word.

hear _____

here _____

7 **Writing Sentences.** On the lines below, write the sentences that you hear.

1. All my ice cream seems to have disappeared.
2. Jean has made many clothes for Kate and me.
3. You need special shears to cut that material.
4. At the beach you must keep your dog on a leash.
5. Dean will teach you how to run this machine.
6. Dale took the middle leaf out of the table.
7. I have been wanting to talk to you all week.
8. We were very weary when we reached Broad Street.
9. We cut through the tunnel to reach Dave's place.
10. Did you hear Mr. Lee speak when he was here last week?

Lesson 12   57

6 Homonyms: *Hear* and *Here*

Help students to discriminate between the homonyms *hear* and *here* by pointing out that *hear* contains the word *ear*.

7 Writing Sentences

Instruct students to write the sentences that you dictate, which are on the replica of the student page. Note any specific errors. Design additional sentences, words, or phrases for specific problems.

Patterns found in these sentences include:
—homonyms (1, 7, 8, and 10)
—adding *-s* or *-es* (1)
—irregular verb forms (2 and 6)
—double consonants in the middle of words (6 and 9)
—possession (9)

Lesson 13
The Word Families *eeze*, *ease*, *eave*, and *ceive*

Objectives

- **Word Families:** Learn to spell words in the *eeze*, *ease*, *eave*, and *ceive* families.
- **Sight Words:** Learn to spell *country*, *touch*, *young*, *hero*, *cheese*, and *sleeve*.
- **Patterns:** Recognize that long *e* can be spelled *e*, *ee*, *ea*, or *ei*. Learn that eCe is an uncommon way to spell long *e*. Review Silent *e* Pattern 1.
- **Dictionary Skills:** Learn the meaning of three words built from the root *ceive*. Use the dictionary to find the correct spelling of long *e* based on phonetic spelling and meaning.
- **Endings:** Practice adding endings to words that end in silent *e*.
- **Writing Sentences:** Practice writing word family and sight words in context.

Sight Words

Teach the sight words using the methods described on pages 9-12 in the introduction to this book.

Point out that *cheese* and *sleeve* have the *ee* spelling for long *e*. Note that *cheese* sounds like the *eeze* family words and that *sleeve* sounds like the *eave* family words.

❶ Listening

Introduce the words in the *eeze* family using the following steps.

1. Say the sound /ēz/ and ask students what letters make the sound in the first group of words.

2. Say the letters *e-e-z-e* and ask students what sound they make.
3. Say the word *breeze* and ask students what letters spell /ēz/ and what letters spell /br/.
4. Say the word *breeze* and ask students what letters spell *breeze*.

Follow the same steps to introduce the words in the *ease*, *eave*, and *ceive* families.

Point out the two pronunciations of *s* in the *ease* family (/z/ as in *tease* and /s/ as in *grease*). Give special attention to *disease*. Many people have a poor visual memory for this word.

❷ Writing Words

Instruct students to write the words that you dictate, which are found on the replica of the student page. Say each word, use it in a phrase or simple sentence, and say the word again.

If students confuse *ee* and *ea* in these words, draw their attention to the correct choice and ask them to make a mental picture of the spelling of the word. Explain that they must place the word in their visual memory. To do this, they should imagine themselves taking a picture of the word, paying special attention to the vowels.

Lesson 13
The Word Families *eeze*, *ease*, *eave*, and *ceive*

Sight Words		
country	young	cheese
touch	hero	sleeve

Word Families

eeze

ease

eave

ceive

❶ Listening

Listen to the sound *eeze* makes in these words.

breeze	freeze	sneeze	squeeze

Listen to the sounds *ease* makes in these words.

ease	tease	cease	crease
disease	please	grease	decrease
displease		release	increase

Listen to the sound *eave* makes in these words.

heave	leave	leaves	weave

Listen to the sound *ceive* makes in these words.

conceive	deceive	receive

❷ Writing Words. On the lines below, write the words that you hear.

1. leaves
2. sneeze
3. teasing
4. freeze
5. displease
6. deceive
7. decrease
8. receive
9. disease

③ Patterns for Spelling Long *e*. Write the words that you hear on the lines below.

1. ___be___   3. ___bead___
2. ___week___   4. ___receive___

Four different ways to spell long *e* are used in the words above. Now write another word for each of the four spellings for long *e*.

1. e _____   3. ea _____
2. ee _____   4. ei _____

④ An Uncommon Pattern: eCe. In Unit 1 you learned many words with the pattern aCe. You learned that a silent *e* at the end of a word makes the *a* long. In this unit you have not learned any eCe words. That is because eCe is not a common spelling for long *e*.

Write the words which your teacher dictates. Each of these is spelled with eCe.

1. ___these___   3. ___Chinese___   5. ___recede___
2. ___theme___   4. ___here___   6. ___complete___

A few other words that contain a long *e* sound follow the VCe syllable pattern, but not very many.

Pattern: Long *e* is spelled eCe in only a few words.

⑤ The Root *ceive*. Several words can be built with the root *ceive*. Look up the words below and write their definitions on the lines provided.

1. receive ___to accept or get something___
2. conceive ___to form an idea; to imagine___
3. deceive ___to mislead or fool someone___

Lesson 13   59

③ Patterns for Spelling Long *e*

This exercise reviews four different ways students have learned to spell the long *e*. Students must recognize that there are a number of ways to spell long *e* and be ready to try a variant spelling if one spelling does not look correct.

④ An Uncommon Pattern: eCe

To spell correctly one must take probabilities into account. Research indicates that one difference between poor spellers and good spellers is that good spellers know both what is possible and what is likely. Although there are many aCe, iCe, and oCe words, eCe words are relatively rare. Other common eCe words include *athlete*, *concede*, *compete*, *extreme*, *gene*, and *scene*.

Help students to understand that, while eCe is a possible way to spell long *e*, it is far more often spelled *e*, *ee*, or *ea*.

⑤ The Root *ceive*

The pattern *ceive* is likewise an uncommon pattern, but it serves as the root for a few useful English words. Encourage students to put the definitions into their own words.

Additional Activity:

Have students use these three words in original sentences.

For more advanced students, discuss the meanings of the prefixes *re-* (back or again), *con-* (together or jointly), and *de-* (reverse or remove).

6 **Dictionary Skills: Finding the Correct Spelling.** Because there are so many different ways to spell long *e*, sometimes you won't remember which one to use. If you can't remember which spelling of long *e* to use, or if the word is new to you, check your dictionary.

Each of the words spelled phonetically below contains the long *e* sound. Use the dictionary to find the correct spelling based on the meaning given. Look first for the *ea* pattern, then for *ee* and *ei*. When you find the spelling that matches the meaning, write the word on the line to the right.

Phonetic Spelling	Meaning	Correct Spelling
1. /brēz/	a gentle wind	breeze
2. /fēst/	a large, elaborate meal	feast
3. /pər sēv/	to become aware of or detect	perceive
4. /spēk/	to talk or converse	speak
5. /spēch/	a talk delivered to an audience	speech
6. /sēs/	to come to an end; stop	cease
7. /sēz/	to take suddenly by force; grab	seize
8. /ē′zē/	needing little effort; not hard	easy
9. /fē′bəl/	weak; without strength	feeble
10. /rĕ sēv/	to take in, acquire, or obtain	receive

Now fill in each word you wrote in the appropriate column below.

ea	*ee*	*ei*
1. feast	1. breeze	1. perceive
2. speak	2. speech	2. seize
3. cease	3. feeble	3. receive
4. easy		

60   Lesson 13

6 Dictionary Skills: Finding the Correct Spelling

This exercise gives students practice in considering the alternative spellings of long *e*. Students must learn to be flexible enough to consider alternative spellings when looking up words in the dictionary. This strategy can avoid the complaint, "How can I look it up if I don't know how to spell it?"

Explain that part of the spelling process is visual monitoring. Students must ask themselves, "Does this word look right?"

Encourage them to try an alternative spelling if their first attempt does not look right to them.

Remind students to use guide words as they try to find the phonetically spelled words.

7 **Reviewing a Pattern.** Fill in the blanks below to review Silent *e* Pattern 1.

The silent *e* at the end of a word is dropped when an ending starting with a

_____vowel_____ is added. The silent *e* is not dropped when the ending starts

with a ___consonant___.

8 **Adding Endings.** Add the endings to the words below. Drop the final silent *e* when necessary.

1. displease + ed   _displeased_
2. cease + less   _ceaseless_
3. sneeze + ing   _sneezing_
4. please + ure   _pleasure_
5. conceive + able   _conceivable_
6. weave + ing   _weaving_
7. deceive + ing   _deceiving_
8. disease + ed   _diseased_
9. receive + able   _receivable_
10. grease + less   _greaseless_

9 **Writing Sentences.** On the lines below, write the sentences that you hear.

1. _Please don't touch the wet paint._
2. _Jean received an increase in her wages._
3. _Please leave the meat in the freezer._
4. _It's not easy to put a crease in this sleeve._
5. _When I was in the country, I saw how cheese is made._
6. _I want you to be completely at ease before we proceed._
7. _As we were raking leaves, the breeze was increasing._
8. _Everyone said Steve was a young hero when he chased the snake away._

Lesson 13   61

7 **Reviewing a Pattern**

Although the word families in this lesson do not follow the **VCe** pattern, they do end in a silent *e*. Point this out to your students when reviewing Silent *e* Pattern 1.

8 **Adding Endings**

Note that the long vowel sound changes when *ure* is added to *please* to form *pleasure*.

9 **Writing Sentences**

Instruct students to write the sentences that you dictate, which are on the replica of the student page. Note any specific errors. Design additional sentences, words, or phrases for specific problems.

Patterns found in these sentences include:
—contractions (1 and 4)
—adding -*s* or -*es* (2 and 7)
—irregular verb forms (5 and 8)
—e**C**e words (6 and 8)
—Silent *e* Pattern 1 (2, 3, 6, 7, and 8)

Lesson 14
The Word Families *ey*, *y*, and *ly*

Objectives

- **Word Families:** Learn to spell words in the *ey*, *y*, and *ly* families.
- **Sight Words:** Learn to spell *father*, *mother*, *parent*, *aunt*, *couple*, and *cousin*.
- **Patterns:** Review double consonants in the middle of two-syllable words.
  Discover that when a word ends in **Cy**, the *y* is changed to *i* before adding any ending except those that start with *i*.
  Learn to change the *y* to *i* and add *-es* to form the plural of words that end in **Cy**.
- **Endings:** Add endings to words that end in **Cy** and to those that don't.
  Make words that end in **Cy** plural.
- **Word Building:** Learn to create adverbs from adjectives by adding *-ly*.
- **Creating Sentences:** Write an original paragraph using word family and sight words.
- **Writing Sentences:** Practice writing word family and sight words in context.

Sight Words

Teach the sight words using the methods described on pages 9-12 in the introduction to this book.

❶ Listening

Introduce the words in the *ey* family using the following steps.

1. Say the sound /ē/ and ask students what letters make the sound in the first group of words.

2. Say the letters *e-y* and ask students what sound they make.
3. Say the word *key* and ask students what letters spell /ē/ and what letter spells /k/.
4. Say the word *key* and ask students what letters spell *key*.

Follow the same steps to introduce the words in the *y* and *ly* families.

Draw attention to the fact that in all these representative family words, the *y* is in the final position. Tell students that if a word with more than one syllable ends with a long *e* sound, the long *e* is probably spelled either *ey* or *y*. It is almost never spelled with an *e*. The few exceptions

are usually words taken from the Greek language. (For more advanced students, you may want to write *apostrophe* and *epitome* on the board and pronounce them.)

Point out that *ly* is a common suffix that we will study in this lesson. Note the retention of the silent *e* in *lately* and *lonely*. These words follow Silent *e* Pattern 1. Note that the *e* is dropped from *true* when *ly* is added. Note also that with *gentle* and *double*, the final *e* is changed to *y* to form *gently* and *doubly*. Tell students that this pattern holds true for most words that end in **Cle** syllables.

Lesson 14
The Word Families *ey*, *y*, and *ly*

Sight Words		
father	parent	couple
mother	aunt	cousin

Word Families

ey

y

ly

❶ Listening

Listen to the sound that *ey* makes in these words.

key	honey	kidney	jersey
hockey	money	journey	volleyball
monkey	valley		

Listen to the sound *y* makes in these words.

any	icy	weary	wavy
shady	greasy	sleepy	bravery
study	greedy	recovery	secretary

Listen to the sound *ly* makes in these words.

jelly	lately	truly	gently
Molly	lonely	daily	doubly
ugly	really		

❷ Writing Words. On the lines below, write the words that you hear.

1. money
2. study
3. valley
4. greasy
5. daily
6. truly
7. lately
8. journey
9. sleepy
10. really
11. speedy
12. recovery

62   Lesson 14

❸ Reviewing a Pattern. In Lesson 12 you learned that if the first syllable of a two-syllable word is a closed syllable, the second syllable usually begins with a consonant. If you do not hear two consonants in the middle of the word, the middle consonant is usually doubled. Write the words your teacher dictates, following this pattern.

1. puppy   3. jolly   5. penny

2. muddy   4. silly   6. funny

❹ Finding a Pattern. Look at the following root words and their endings.

Root	Ending	New Word	Root	Ending	New Word
1. marry	+ ed	married	5. cry	+ ing	crying
2. lazy	+ est	laziest	6. copy	+ ing	copying
3. easy	+ ly	easily	7. carry	+ ing	carrying
4. penny	+ less	penniless	8. vary	+ ing	varying

The letter before the final *y* in the root words is a ___consonant___.
                                  (consonant *or* vowel)

What happens to the final *y* when the first four endings are added?

   The *y* changes to *i.*

What happens to the final *y* when *-ing* is added?   Nothing happens.

> **Pattern:** When adding a suffix to a word that ends in **C***y*, change the *y* to *i* unless the suffix begins with *i.*

❺ Adding Endings to Words That End in *y*. Add the endings to the words below.

1. copy + er   copier
2. journey + ed   journeyed
3. sleepy + ly   sleepily
4. study + ing   studying
5. easy + est   easiest
6. sorry + er   sorrier
7. rainy + est   rainiest
8. marry + ing   marrying
9. greedy + ly   greedily
10. jockey + ed   jockeyed

Lesson 14   63

❷ Writing Words

Instruct students to write the words that you dictate, which are found on the replica of the student page. Say each word, use it in a phrase or simple sentence, and say the word again.

❸ Reviewing a Pattern

The dictated words follow the pattern of having their middle consonants doubled and also end in long *e* spelled *y.*

❹ Finding a Pattern

In this exercise, students discover that we change *y* to *i* when adding suffixes to words ending in **C***y*, unless the suffix begins with *i.*

❺ Adding Endings to Words That End in *y*

This exercise gives students practice in applying the pattern learned in Exercise 4. Be sure that students do not change the *y* to *i* in *journeyed* or *jockeyed*. If they do, remind them that the *y* to *i* rule is only for words that end in a consonant plus *y.*

Additional Activity:

Draw students' attention to the *-er* suffix in *sorrier* and the *-est* suffix in *easiest* and *rainiest*. Point out that these suffixes are added to adjectives to make the comparative and superlative forms. They indicate *more* and *most.*

6 **Discovering Another Pattern.** Look at the pairs of singular and plural words below.

Singular	Plural	Singular	Plural	Singular	Plural
cake	cakes	key	keys	baby	babies
team	teams	valley	valleys	penny	pennies

What letter is added to make most words plural? _____ s _____

What happens to words that end in a consonant plus *y* when they become plural?

_____ The *y* changes to *i* and *es* is added. _____

Pattern: To make a word ending in **C***y* plural, change the *y* to *i* and add *-es*.

Following the pattern above, write the plurals of these words.

1. city _____ cities _____   4. jelly _____ jellies _____
2. lily _____ lilies _____   5. injury _____ injuries _____
3. puppy _____ puppies _____   6. mystery _____ mysteries _____

7 **Word Building with *-ly*.** When *-ly* is added to some adjectives (words that describe nouns), the new words that are formed are adverbs (words that describe verbs, adjectives, or other adverbs). Study the examples below.

The *graceful* couple danced all evening. (*Graceful* is an adjective.)
The couple danced *gracefully* all evening. (*Gracefully* is an adverb.)

Create adverbs from the adjectives below by adding *-ly* to them.

1. safe _____ safely _____   6. hasty _____ hastily _____
2. easy _____ easily _____   7. weary _____ wearily _____
3. fair _____ fairly _____   8. lone _____ lonely _____
4. brave _____ bravely _____   9. late _____ lately _____
5. strange _____ strangely _____   10. sleepy _____ sleepily _____

64   Lesson 14

6 **Discovering Another Pattern**

In this exercise, students discover how to form the plural of words that end in **C***y*. Again, this pattern does not pertain to words ending in *ey*.

7 **Word Building with *-ly***

The point of this exercise is to draw students' attention to the fact that adverbs can be formed by adding *-ly* to adjectives.

If students are not familiar with the terms *adjective* and *adverb*, give them a few more example sentences. Do not worry if they don't remember these terms.

Be sure students change the *y* to *i* before adding *-ly* in numbers 2, 6, 7, and 10.

8 **Creating Sentences.** On a separate sheet of paper, write a paragraph describing the scene below. Use some of the following family and sight words in your sentences.

father	cousin	journey	hear
mother	couple	reach	clear
parents	yearly	appear	shady
aunt	feast	leave	volleyball

9 **Writing Sentences.** On the lines below, write the sentences that you hear.

1. Emily can't locate the keys to her car.
2. Amy's parents will be here presently.
3. How many pennies does Daisy have in her piggy bank?
4. The mother monkey was carrying her baby on her back.
5. A couple of people on our volleyball team also play hockey.
6. Would you prefer honey or jelly on your peanut butter sandwich?
7. Did your mother and father receive the money you sent last week?
8. My aunt was lonely after my cousin got married and moved away.

Lesson 14   65

---

8 Creating Sentences

Discuss the illustration with students before they begin to write. Encourage them to use as many long *e* and sight words as they can.

If students ask how to spell a word that they have not studied, encourage them to look it up in the dictionary.

Evaluate spelling patterns and words already learned. Look specifically to see if students are able to apply patterns learned. Note any pattern of errors in this spontaneous writing sample.

Do not be overly concerned about misspellings in words or patterns not yet studied. This will encourage students to risk more and write more sophisticated sentences.

9 Writing Sentences

Instruct students to write the sentences that you dictate, which are on the replica of the student page. Note any specific errors. Design additional sentences, words, or phrases for specific problems.

Patterns found in these sentences include:
—adding -*s* or -*es* (1, 2, and 3)
—contractions (1)
—adding -*ly* to make adverbs (2 and 8)
—possession (2)
—double consonants in the middle of words (3, 4, 5, 6, and 8)
—changing *y* to *i* pattern (3, 4, and 8)

Review of Unit 2
The Long *e*

Objectives

- **Syllable Types:** Review the attributes of five syllable types. Categorize and identify syllables by type.
- **Writing by Syllables:** Write dictated words by syllables.
- **Patterns for Spelling Long *e*:** Review six ways to spell long *e*.
- **Dictionary Skills:** Practice using guide words to find words in the dictionary.
  Learn the meanings of some two-, three-, and four-syllable words and use them to complete sentences.
  Use irregular forms of verbs to complete sentences.
- **Homonyms:** Review homonyms with the *ee* and *ea* digraphs.
- **Word Building:** Build words by combining syllables.
- **Adding Endings:** Add endings to words that end in **C***y* and in silent *e*; add *-ly* to adjectives.
- **Writing Sentences:** Practice writing word family and sight words in context.
- **Puzzle:** Review long *e* family words and sight words by completing a crossword puzzle.

Review of Unit 2
The Long *e*

1 **Reviewing Syllable Types.** You have learned five syllable types in this unit: closed (C), open (O), consonant + *le* (**C**le), vowel-consonant-*e* (**VC**e), and double vowel (D).

Part A. Fill in the blanks below to review the five syllable types.

1. A closed syllable ends with a ___consonant___ and has a ___short___ vowel.
2. An open syllable ends with a ___vowel___, which is usually ___long___.
3. A consonant + *le* syllable (**C**le) usually comes at the ___end___ of a word.
4. The first vowel in a vowel-consonant-*e* syllable (**VC**e) is ___long___ and the *e* is ___silent___.
5. A double vowel syllable has ___two___ vowels together that make ___one___ sound.

Part B. Place the following syllables under the correct heading.

ain	re	son	cle	dle
ba	sim	tle	reed	ane
com	ade	ite	fe	ceal

Closed
1. com
2. sim
3. son

Open
1. ba
2. re
3. fe

Cle
1. tle
2. cle
3. dle

VCe
1. ade
2. ite
3. ane

Double Vowel
1. ain
2. reed
3. ceal

66   Review of Unit 2

1 Reviewing Syllable Types

Exercise 1 reviews the five syllable types covered in Unit 2. The primary attributes of each type are reviewed in Part A. In Part B, students are asked to categorize representative syllables under the correct headings. Then in Part C they are asked to identify specific syllables by type. Note any difficulties students appear to have with a particular type of syllable.

Part C. On the line beside each of the following syllables, write what kind of syllable it is.

1. ple	_Cle_	5. main	_D_	9. e	_O_
2. gel	_C_	6. mu	_O_	10. ale	_VCe_
3. us	_C_	7. ble	_Cle_	11. pire	_VCe_
4. lete	_VCe_	8. ceed	_D_	12. ba	_O_

② **Writing Words by Syllables.** Write the words that you hear one syllable at a time. Then write the whole word on the line at the right.

First Syllable	Second Syllable	Third Syllable	Whole Word
1. pre	heat		preheat
2. muf	fle		muffle
3. in	com	plete	incomplete
4. ab	so	lute	absolute
5. re	fin	ish	refinish

③ **Patterns for Spelling Long e.** On the lines below, write the words that you hear.

1. legal	3. conceal	5. study
2. freedom	4. money	6. these

Six different ways to spell long *e* are used in the words you wrote. Now write another word for each of the six spellings for long *e*.

1. e _____   4. ey _____
2. ee _____ 5. y _____
3. ea _____ 6. eCe _____

② **Writing Words by Syllables**

Dictate each word by syllables, emphasizing the syllables. Then pronounce the whole word normally. Remind students that the number of blanks indicates the number of syllables in the word. If students have difficulty with any of these words, help them to isolate the problem syllable and listen to it.

③ **Patterns for Spelling Long e**

In this exercise, the following patterns that produce long *e* are reviewed: *e*, *ee*, *ea*, *ey*, *y*, and eCe. Remind students that *ey* and *y* occur at the end of words and that eCe is an uncommon pattern.

4 **Dictionary Skills: Guide Words.** Below are sets of guide words that might be found on dictionary pages. Decide if the words listed below them would appear on the dictionary page that has those guide words. Underline each word that would be found on that page.

1. **headache — hearken**

   hear   heal   here   heel

2. **bear — because**

   beet   bean   been   beat

3. **stay — stencil**

   steal   seam   seem   steel

4. **chatter — cheer**

   cheep   cheek   cheat   cheap

5 **Homonyms.** Write either *ea* or *ee* in the blanks below depending on the definition given. Use your dictionary to check your answers.

1. the opposite of strong   w_e_a_k

2. a dark red vegetable   b_e_e_t

3. to listen with the ear   h_e_a_r

4. to run away   fl_e_e_

5. a strong metal   st_e_e_l

6. a group working together   t_e_a_m

7. return to health   h_e_a_l

8. authentic   r_e_a_l

9. the skin of a fruit   p_e_e_l

10. not expensive   ch_e_a_p

6 **Word Building.** Add a syllable from Column 2 to a syllable in Column 1 to make a word. Write the new words on the lines provided. Use each syllable only once. The first one has been done to get you started.

Column 1	Column 2		New Word
√be	fee	1.	began
nee	teen	2.	needle
cof	ceed	3.	coffee
fif	√gan	4.	fifteen
suc	dle	5.	succeed

4 **Dictionary Skills: Guide Words**

This exercise reviews the procedure for using guide words to determine if a specific word will be found on a particular page in a dictionary. If students are having trouble with this procedure, you may want to provide additional practice by developing other exercises patterned after this one.

5 **Homonyms**

Remind students that a number of homonym pairs contain long *e*. In this exercise students must choose whether the long *e* is spelled with *ee* or *ea* based on the definition given. They should use their dictionaries to verify their answers.

6 **Word Building**

In this exercise, students are asked to combine syllables to form words. Tell students to check off the syllables as they use them, to ensure that each syllable is used only once.

7 **Adding Endings.** Add the endings to the words below.

1. sick + ly	sickly	10. lazy + ly	lazily
2. muddy + est	muddiest	11. secret + ly	secretly
3. name + less	nameless	12. copy + ing	copying
4. baby + ing	babying	13. dangerous + ly	dangerously
5. parade + ed	paraded	14. escape + ed	escaped
6. penny + s *or* es	pennies	15. silly + er	sillier
7. legal + ly	legally	16. race + ing	racing
8. happy + ly	happily	17. puppy + s *or* es	puppies
9. price + less	priceless	18. sudden + ly	suddenly

8 **Dictionary Skills: Using Words with Many Syllables.** Complete the following sentences by filling in one of the words below. Use your dictionary to find the meanings of the words when you need to.

absolute	confiscated	grapple	mayonnaise	reignite
compensate	established	magnetic	preheat	stagnate

1. That company was __established__ in 1901.
2. If a fire isn't completely out, it can __reignite__.
3. How can I __compensate__ you for the fine job you did?
4. Would you like mustard or __mayonnaise__ on your sandwich?
5. The water in the pond will __stagnate__ as it dries up.
6. A compass has a __magnetic__ needle which points north.
7. The police __confiscated__ the illegal weapons.
8. When the electricity went off, the room was in __absolute__ darkness.
9. A meeting was called to __grapple__ with the problem of absenteeism.
10. You should __preheat__ the oven before you start to bake the cake.

Review of Unit 2   69

7 **Adding Endings**

Several patterns for adding endings are reviewed in this exercise: adding -*ly* to adjectives to form adverbs, changing the *y* to *i* in words ending in **C**y, and Silent *e* Pattern 1. You may want to review these patterns before students do this exercise. Note any difficulties students have with a particular pattern.

8 **Dictionary Skills: Using Words with Many Syllables**

The words in this exercise are taken from the Writing Words by Syllables exercises in this unit. This exercise gives students the opportunity to use these words in context. They will need to look up the dictionary definitions for unfamiliar words.

9 Dictionary Skills: Irregular Verbs. Fill in the blanks in the sentences below with the correct form of the verb in parentheses. Look up the verbs in a dictionary if you need to find the correct form.

1. (leave) Have all your guests _____left_____ so soon?
2. (weep) Lee nearly _____wept_____ with joy when he won the scholarship.
3. (hear) Have you _____heard_____ from Beatrice lately?
4. (beat) The volleyball team has been _____beaten_____ only once this year.
5. (lead) The guide _____led_____ us down the path to the bottom of the canyon.
6. (mean) I _____meant_____ to tell you about that yesterday, but I forgot.
7. (steal) Steve has _____stolen_____ more bases than any other player on the team.
8. (teach) Mr. Teeter _____taught_____ English for twenty-five years.
9. (deal) Before Eileen _____dealt_____ the cards, Jean served the dessert.
10. (seek) The board members have _____sought_____ a solution to that problem for weeks.

10 Writing Sentences. On the lines below, write the sentences that you hear.

1. How did Dean react when he saw you really meant it?
2. One of Steve's kidneys is weak and may be diseased.
3. Jean nearly wept with happiness when her team beat the seniors.
4. Emily carried the clothes to the machine and just left them there.
5. I hear your cousin is marrying Gail's secretary in two weeks.
6. Pete will need to complete that job before he leaves.
7. Although we had enough coffee for everyone, we ran out of cream and sugar.
8. Doreen was especially pleased to receive three copies of Mrs. Green's book.

9 Dictionary Skills: Irregular Verbs

These are all verbs from Unit 2 word families that have irregular principal parts. Encourage students to use their dictionaries to look up the principal parts if they need to. If they are keeping a table of irregular verbs in their notebooks, have them add these to the list.

10 Writing Sentences

Instruct students to write the sentences that you dictate, which are on the replica of the student page. Note any specific errors. Design additional sentences, words, or phrases for specific problems.

Patterns found in these sentences include:
—irregular verb forms (1, 3, and 4)
—adding -ly to form adverbs (1 and 3)
—adding -s or -es (2, 3, 5, 6, and 8)
—possession (2, 5, and 8)
—Silent e Pattern 1 (2 and 8)
—eCe pattern (2 and 6)
—changing y to i pattern (3, 4, 5, and 8)

```
 1        2        3       4   5        6        7
 C  O  L  O  R  E  D      S  C  R  E  A  M
 O     E        I        O     Q        O
 8
 N  E  A  R     S        U     U        N
 C     D     9  T        S     A        E
            10 E  S  P  E  C  I  A  L  L  Y
 I           E  P        N
11 12          13      14 15      16
 V  O  L  U  N  T  E  E  R   O  W  E  S
 E  E        A     E        E        E
           17             18     19
    S  U  G  A  R  L  E  S  S      M  E
20
 H  I  S     E        L     H        D
 E        21 R  E  A  D  S  22 E  A  S  Y
```

Across

1. Dyed; used crayons
4. A loud, shrill cry
8. Opposite of far
10. Particularly: She is ____ good in math.
11. A person who offers free help
14. Is in debt: He ____ me a dollar.
17. Without a kind of sweetener: ____ gum
19. "____, myself, and I"
20. Belonging to him
21. Gets meaning from printed words
22. Not hard

Down

1. To think of or imagine something
2. The opposite of follow
3. Vanish: How could he ____ without a trace?
5. The child of your aunt or uncle
6. Having the same value as something else: Does 1 plus 1 ____ 2?
7. This is used to buy things.
9. Someone older than twelve but younger than twenty
12. An ending meaning "without"
13. These can be found on fishing poles and movie projectors.
15. You and I
16. Full of small pits: These grapes are ____.
18. He, ____, and it
20. The opposite of she

(11) **Crossword Puzzle**

Tell students that most of the answers for this crossword puzzle are long *e* words or sight words from Unit 2. The clues are mostly definitions that rely on the students' body of general knowledge.

Allow students to use a dictionary if they want to. If necessary, supply them with the following list of answer words and tell them to cross off words as they use them.

colored	money
conceive	near
cousin	owes
disappear	reads
easy	reels
equal	scream
especially	seedy
he	she
his	sugarless
lead	teenager
less	volunteer
me	we

Unit 2 Tests

We recommend that you test your students on the word family and sight words from Unit 2 before going on. The following are suggested lists of representative family words and sight words from Unit 2. You may want to substitute other words to meet the needs of your students.

Dictate each word and use it in a simple sentence. Students should be able to spell **90 percent of these words correctly.**

Family Words	Sight Words
1. eat	1. owe
2. feel	2. double
3. read	3. enough
4. beyond	4. busy
5. each	5. tongue
6. meeting	6. cousin
7. cream	7. prove
8. please	8. touch
9. between	9. course
10. reason	10. rough
11. freedom	11. father
12. appear	12. although
13. money	13. else
14. proceed	14. length
15. truly	15. young
16. weekend	16. country
17. speak	17. mother
18. speech	18. clothes
19. leaves	19. purpose
20. conceal	20. especially

Lesson 15
The Word Families *ime*, *ibe*, *ike*, *ice*, *ipe*, and *ile*

Objectives

- **Word Families:** Learn to spell words in the *ime*, *ibe*, *ike*, *ice*, *ipe*, and *ile* families.
- **Sight Words:** Learn to spell *question*, *answer*, *die*, *dye*, *board*, *bored*, *both*, and *rhyme*.
- **Homonyms:** Learn to use correctly *board/bored* and *die/dye*.
- **Creating Sentences:** Use homonyms in original sentences.
- **Syllable Types:** Review five types of syllables. Write words with iCe syllables.
- **Endings:** Add endings to words that end in silent *e*.
- **Root Words:** Find root words by removing endings.
- **Spelling Names:** Spell unfamiliar names by using syllable types.
- **Dictionary Skills:** Locate names in an alphabetized list.
- **Writing Sentences:** Practice writing word family and sight words in context.

Sight Words

Teach the sight words using the methods described on pages 9-12 in the introduction to this book.

Remind students that *q* is always followed by *u* in English words, as in the word *question*. Point out the silent *w* in *answer*. Students who tend to rely most heavily on auditory strategies to remember the spelling of words will benefit from mispronouncing the word to include the *w* sound when they are spelling *answer*. Point out the two pairs of homonyms: *die/dye* and *board/bored*, and the silent *h* in *rhyme*.

Discuss the word *both* as an example of a word that doesn't follow normal patterns.

T: What kind of syllable is *both*?
S: Closed.

Lesson 15
The Word Families *ime*, *ibe*, *ike*, *ice*, *ipe*, and *ile*

Sight Words

| question | die | board | both |
| answer | dye | bored | rhyme |

Word Families

1 Listening

ime

Listen to the sound *ime* makes in these words.

dime	time	prime
chime	overtime	grime
crime	sometimes	slime

ibe

Listen to the sound *ibe* makes in these words.

| bribe | tribe | describe | prescribe |

ike

Listen to the sound *ike* makes in these words.

| like | bike | dike | spike |
| alike | hike | Mike | strike |

ice

Listen to the sound *ice* makes in these words.

ice	rice	device	slice
mice	price	advice	sacrifice
nice	twice		

ipe

Listen to the sound *ipe* makes in these words.

| ripe | wipe | stripe |
| gripe | swipe | pipeline |

ile

Listen to the sound *ile* makes in these words.

| file | mile | tile | awhile |
| pile | smile | while | meanwhile |

T: What vowel sound do closed syllables usually have?
S: Short.
T: What is the vowel sound in *both*?
S: Long *o*.
T: So *both* doesn't follow the normal pattern. That is why it is a sight word.

1 Listening

Introduce the words in the *ime* family using the following steps.

1. Say the sound /īm/ and ask students what letters make the sound.
2. Say the letters *i-m-e* and ask students what sound they make.

3. Say the word *dime* and ask students what letters spell /īm/ and what letter spells /d/.
4. Say the word *dime* and ask students what letters spell *dime*.

Follow the same steps to introduce the words in the *ibe*, *ike*, *ice*, *ipe*, and *ile* families.

Review the **VCe** syllable type and point out that the word families in this lesson are all of this type. Point out the schwa in *alike* and *awhile*. Note that the *a* in both of these words is an unaccented open syllable.

2 **Writing Words.** On the lines below, write the words that you hear.

1. hiking   4. advice   7. timekeeper

2. dimes   5. ripe   8. describe

3. likely   6. filing   9. meanwhile

3 **Dictionary Skills: Homonyms.** Look up the definitions of the following sight words and write them on the lines.

1. board   a long, thin piece of wood; a committee that directs an organization

2. bored   drilled a hole; tired because you've lost interest

3. dye   to color something

4. die   to stop living; a metal block for stamping or cutting

Now write a sentence using a form of each of these words.

1. board _____

2. bored _____

3. dye _____

4. die _____

4 **Syllable Types.** The five types of syllables you have studied so far are listed below. An example of each type is given. Write another example of each type of syllable on the lines provided.

Syllable Type	Example	Your Example
1. Closed	bit	rim
2. Open	li	bi
3. Cle	tle	dle
4. VCe	ime	ice
5. Double Vowel	tain	deed

Lesson 15   73

Additional Activity:

The family words in this lesson present a good opportunity to review compound words. Have students tell you what two words make up *overtime*, *sometimes*, *pipeline*, and *meanwhile*. Have students look up *time* in their dictionaries and write down all the compound words they find that start with *time*. Have them note whether the compounds are closed, hyphenated, or open.

Ask students if they can think of compounds using other word families from this lesson. Have them use their dictionaries to see if they are closed, hyphenated, or open compounds.

2 **Writing Words**

Instruct students to write the words that you dictate, which are found on the replica of the student page. Say each word, use it in a phrase or simple sentence, and say the word again.

3 **Dictionary Skills: Homonyms**

With the exception of *dye*, the words in this exercise all have multiple meanings. Encourage students to find two separate definitions of the other three words, as in the sample answers on the replica of the student page. Students can then select one of the definitions for each word to use in their sentences.

Point out that students will have to look up the root word *bore* to find *bored*. Since the *-ed* ending indicates an action that happened in the past, remind students that their definitions should be written in the past tense, also.

Additional Activity:

Ask students to find the dictionary guide words for each of these homonyms.

4 **Syllable Types**

This exercise reviews the five types of syllables students learned in Unit 2. The answers on the replica of the student page are examples. Accept all correct responses.

5 **The VCe Syllable Type.** A vowel-consonant-*e* syllable ends in a silent *e*. This silent *e* usually causes the vowel to be long. On the lines below, write nine words which follow the **VCe** pattern and have a long *i* sound.

1. _____   4. _____   7. _____
2. _____   5. _____   8. _____
3. _____   6. _____   9. _____

6 **Review of Silent *e* Pattern 1.** The silent *e* at the end of a word is dropped when adding an ending that starts with a vowel. When the ending starts with a consonant, the silent *e* is not dropped. Add the endings to the words below.

1. mile + s   miles
2. tribe + al   tribal
3. price + less   priceless
4. bike + ed   biked
5. pipe + ing   piping
6. like + ly   likely

7. time + less   timeless
8. nice + est   nicest
9. smile + ing   simling
10. like + ness   likeness
11. wipe + er   wiper
12. describe + ed described

7 **Finding Root Words.** Write the root word for each of the words below.

1. planning   plan
2. striped   stripe
3. bikes   bike
4. biggest   big
5. gushes   gush
6. smiling   smile

7. filed   file
8. puppies   puppy
9. grimy   grime
10. hiker   hike
11. sliced   slice
12. striking   strike

74   Lesson 15

5 The VCe Syllable Type

If students have difficulty generating the nine words on their own, remind them that the words in the listening exercise are all **VCe** words.

6 Review of Silent *e* Pattern 1

Note any problems students may still be having when adding endings to words that end in silent *e*. Design reinforcement activities for those students as needed.

7 Finding Root Words

This exercise reverses the procedure for adding endings. Review the term *root word* before students begin.

The following patterns are reviewed in this exercise:

- Doubling Pattern 1 from Book 1 of this series
- Silent *e* Pattern 1
- adding -*es* to words ending in *s*, *x*, *z*, *ch*, and *sh*, also from Book 1 of this series
- changing the *y* to *i* before adding endings to words that end in C*y*.

Note any particular areas of difficulty your students have and develop reinforcement activities if necessary.

8 **Writing Unfamiliar Names.** On the lines below, write the last names that your teacher dictates. The types of syllables you have studied will help you to spell the names.

1. Updike
2. Stapleton
3. Collins
4. Aiken
5. Price
6. Hickle
7. Beecher
8. Romano
9. Tassone
10. Abrams
11. Cadwell
12. Gilbo

9 **Locating Names in a Directory.** Below is a directory of doctors in a physicians' office building. Underline the names from Exercise 8.

Abrams	Bostic	Gale	Miles	Seeley
Aiken	Cadwell	Gilbo	Patrick	Stapleton
Alexander	Case	Hickle	Price	Sullivan
Bailey	Collins	Johnson	Regan	Tassone
Beecher	Deaver	Keene	Riley	Updike
Bidwell	Eaton	Lacy	Romano	Weeks

10 **Writing Sentences.** On the lines below, write the sentences that you hear.

1. If it doesn't rain, those rice plants will die.
2. When Eileen dyed her hair, it came out green.
3. Can you think of a word that rhymes with *orange*?
4. Mr. Price was describing how the device was made.
5. If you smiled sometimes, you wouldn't seem so bored.
6. I like both of those bikes, but I think this one is nicer.
7. Mike cleaned the board twice to get off all the grime.
8. Sometimes parents make a lot of sacrifices for their children.
9. The men were griping about having to stay overtime.
10. It wasn't easy to answer all the questions in the time we were given.

Lesson 15   75

---

8 **Writing Unfamiliar Names**

In this exercise, students review the five types of syllables they have learned by writing surnames. Dictate the names by syllables, exaggerating the pronunciation slightly. Avoid any schwas. For example, pronounce the short *e* in the name *Aiken*. If students have trouble spelling these names, suggest they write them by syllables.

Pay special attention to students' performance on this exercise. They will not be relying on visual memory but must apply their knowledge of word families, syllables, and phonics.

Students should realize that sometimes there are alternative spellings possible. For example, *Beecher* could be spelled *Beacher* and *Gilbo* could be spelled *Gilboe* or *Gilbow*. Accept any alternative spellings which follow regular patterns.

9 **Locating Names in a Directory**

This exercise permits students to use scanning skills to locate the names, a frequently needed skill. Discuss how students completed this task. Did they search for names by letters, by syllables, or by the entire name? This will give you a clue as to the extent that individual students are able to retain words with which they are not familiar.

After they have underlined the names in the directory, have them check the spellings against the names they wrote in Exercise 8.

10 **Writing Sentences**

Instruct students to write the sentences that you dictate, which are on the replica of the student page. Note any specific errors. Design additional sentences, words, or phrases for specific problems.

Patterns found in these sentences include:
—homonyms (1, 2, 4, 5, and 7)
—adding -*s* or -*es* (1, 3, 5, 6, 8, and 10)
—contractions (1, 5, and 10)
—irregular verb forms (2, 4, and 10)
—Silent *e* Pattern 1 (4, 5, 6, and 9)

In response to number 3, you might wish to point out that there are no English words that rhyme exactly with the word *orange*.

Lesson 16

The Word Families *ine*, *ire*, *ide*, *ite*, *ife*, and *ive*

		Sight Words	
cough	route	shoulder	
court	group	thorough	

Word Families

① Listening

ine

Listen to the sound *ine* makes in these words.

dine	fine	spine	shine
line	define	whine	sunshine
mine	decline	combine	Valentine

ire

Listen to the sound *ire* makes in these words.

fire	tire	bonfire	admire
hire	entire	inquire	desire
wire	retired	require	expire

ide

Listen to the sound *ide* makes in these words.

hide	beside	ride	tide
side	decide	bride	slide
wide	divide	pride	provide

ite

Listen to the sound *ite* makes in these words.

bite	quite	ignite	excite
kite	unite	invite	excitement
white	write	recite	unexcited

ife

Listen to the sound *ife* makes in these words.

life	knife	wife	lifetime

ive

Listen to the sound *ive* makes in these words.

live	drive	hive	
alive	driveway	thrive	

76   Lesson 16

Lesson 16
The Word Families *ine*, *ire*, *ide*, *ite*, *ife*, and *ive*

Objectives

- **Word Families:** Learn to spell words in the *ine*, *ire*, *ide*, *ite*, *ife*, and *ive* families.
- **Sight Words:** Learn to spell *cough*, *court*, *route*, *group*, *shoulder*, and *thorough*. Use the sight words to complete sentences.
- **Word Building:** Add word families to initial consonants to form words.
  Add suffixes to root words.
- **Pattern:** Learn that the plurals of some words that end in *f* or *fe* are formed by changing the *f* or *fe* to *v* and adding *-es*.
- **Dictionary Skills:** Find the principal parts of designated irregular verbs.
- **Creating Sentences:** Write an original paragraph using word family and sight words.
- **Writing Sentences:** Practice writing word family and sight words in context.

Sight Words

Teach the sight words using the methods described on pages 9-12 in the introduction to this book.

All of the sight words for this lesson have the vowel combination *ou*. Several pronunciations of *ou* are represented. Compare these pronunciations with some of the other sight words that also contain the *ou* combination. For instance, compare the pronunciation of *cough* with that of *dough*, *rough*, and *tough*. Compare *court* with *course*. Compare *thorough* with *through*, a sight word from Book 1. These two words are often confused.

① Listening

Introduce the words in the *ine* family using the following steps.

1. Say the sound /īn/ and ask students what letters make the sound.
2. Say the letters *i-n-e* and ask students what sound they make.
3. Say the word *dine* and ask students what letters spell /īn/ and what letter spells /d/.
4. Say the word *dine* and ask students what letters spell *dine*.

Follow the same steps to introduce the words in the *ire*, *ide*, *ite*, *ife*, and *ive* families.

2 Writing Words. On the lines below, write the words that you hear.

1. write
2. vine
3. lifetime
4. alive
5. invite
6. divided
7. define
8. entirely
9. providing

3 Word Building. Add *ine, ire, ide, ite, ife,* or *ive* to each of the consonants to make a word. Do not make the same word twice.

1. f ine
2. f ive
3. h ide
4. h ive
5. l ife
6. l ive
7. m ine
8. t ire
9. wr ite

4 Using Sight Words. Use one of the sight words from this lesson in each of the following sentences.

1. A large _____group_____ of students was watching the game.
2. Gary's son has had a paper _____route_____ for two years.
3. The doctor gave him a _____thorough_____ examination.
4. Mary's recent cold left her with a bad _____cough_____.
5. Dave injured his _____shoulder_____ and can't pitch today.
6. Mike will meet us at the tennis _____court_____ at five o'clock.

5 Forming the Plurals of Words That End in *f* or *fe*. Some words that end in *f* or *fe* are made plural by changing the *f* or *fe* to *v* and adding *-es*. Make these words plural by following this pattern. The first one has been done to get you started.

1. wife — wives
2. life — lives
3. knife — knives
4. leaf — leaves
5. half — halves
6. calf — calves
7. self — selves
8. wolf — wolves

Lesson 16   77

❷ Writing Words

Instruct students to write the words that you dictate, which are found on the replica of the student page. Say each word, use it in a phrase or simple sentence, and say the word again.

❸ Word Building

Have students add one of the word families to each consonant or digraph to make a word. Encourage them to use all of the word families at least once. The answers given on the replica of the student page are examples. Accept all correctly spelled words.

❹ Using Sight Words

This exercise gives students the opportunity to use the sight words in context.

❺ Forming the Plurals of Words That End in *f* or *fe*

Explain to students that in a number of words that end in *f* or *fe*, the *f* or *fe* is changed to *v* before adding *-es* to form the plural. When students are forming the plural of a word ending in *f* or *fe*, they should say the plural aloud. If they hear a /v/, then they know they must change the *f* to a *v*. This exercise gives them practice with this pattern.

6 **Word Building.** Use each root word to make three more words by adding three of these endings: *-ed, -ment, -ing, -less, -er,* or *-s.* Use each ending at least once.

1. excite	excited	excitement	exciting
2. unite	united	uniting	unites
3. time	timeless	timer	timed
4. retire	retired	retirement	retiring
5. dine	dined	dining	diner
6. write	writing	writer	writes
7. fine	fined	finer	fines
8. wire	wired	wireless	wiring

Now make the two new words below.

1. excite + ed + ly ___excitedly___   2. decide + ed + ly ___decidedly___

7 **Dictionary Skills: Irregular Verbs.** Look up the following irregular verbs in the dictionary, and write the different forms in the appropriate columns.

Present Tense	Past Tense	*Have, Has,* or *Had* + Verb	*-ing* Form of Verb
1. ride	rode	ridden	riding
2. strike	struck	stricken/struck	striking
3. bite	bit	bitten/bit	biting
4. write	wrote	written	writing
5. hide	hid	hidden/hid	hiding
6. drive	drove	driven	driving

6 Word Building

In this exercise, students form a number of words by choosing three endings for each of the root words.

Pay special attention to number 5, *dine.* Students sometimes double the *n* to make *dinner.* Also pay attention to number 6, *write.* If a student writes *writting*, review the procedure for adding endings to words that end with silent *e.*

The answers on the replica of the student page are examples. Accept all correctly spelled words.

At the end of the exercise, students are asked to add both *-ed* and *-ly* to *excite* and *decide.* Explain that sometimes we add more than one ending to a word.

Additional Activity:

Challenge students to write other words by adding the endings given or their own endings to other root words.

7 Dictionary Skills: Irregular Verbs

Review the principal parts of verbs before students begin this exercise. If students are listing irregular verbs in their notebooks, have them add these when they finish the exercise.

Two forms of the past participles of *strike, bite,* and *hide* are listed in most dictionaries. Accept either form.

8 **Creating Sentences.** On a separate piece of paper, write a paragraph about the picture below. Use some of the following long *i* words in your sentences.

hire	life	line	fine
time	lifetime	knife	like
overtime	pride	nice	beside
retire	invite	smile	excitement

Congratulations on Your Retirement

9 **Writing Sentences.** On the lines below, write the sentences that you hear.

1. This is an exciting time to be alive.
2. A volleyball court has a net in the middle.
3. Should Mike be taking something for his bad cough?
4. The group will decide which route to take.
5. Pete is tired because his job requires so much overtime.
6. The men got special valentines for their wives.
7. Lee dislocated his shoulder when his car was sideswiped.
8. We drove past the path because it was thoroughly hidden by bushes.

Lesson 16   79

8 Creating Sentences

Discuss the illustration with students before they begin to write. Encourage them to use as many long *i* and sight words as they can.

If students ask how to spell a word that they have not studied, encourage them to look it up in the dictionary. Remember that errors in words that haven't been studied shouldn't be treated negatively. Point out any parts of the word that are spelled correctly and praise the effort.

9 Writing Sentences

Instruct students to write the sentences that you dictate, which are on the replica of the student page. Note any specific errors. Design additional sentences, words, or phrases for specific problems.

Patterns found in these sentences include:
—Silent *e* Pattern 1 (1, 3, 5, and 7)
—double consonants in the middle of words (2 and 8)
—adding -*s* or -*es* (5, 6, and 8)
—changing *f* or *fe* to *v* (6)
—irregular verb forms (8)
—adding -*ly* to form adverbs (8)

The Word Families *ise*, *ize*, and *y*

<table>
<tr><td colspan="4">Sight Words</td></tr>
<tr><td>liquid</td><td>weigh</td><td>ounce</td><td>oz.</td></tr>
<tr><td>fluid</td><td>weight</td><td>pound</td><td>lb.</td></tr>
</table>

Word Families

ise

1 **Listening**

Listen to the sound *ise* makes in these words.

rise	wise	surprise	despise
arise	advise	supervise	disguise
	revise	advertise	exercise

ize

Listen to the sound *ize* makes in these words.

size	realize	memorize	recognize
prize	criticize	alphabetize	

y

Listen to the sound *y* makes in these words.

cry	fry	deny	apply
dry	shy	rely	supply
try	why	reply	identify

2 **Writing Words.** On the lines below, write the words that you hear.

1. size
2. wise
3. cry
4. deny
5. realize
6. advising
7. applying
8. exercises
9. memorize
10. identify
11. criticize
12. supervise

Lesson 17

The Word Families *ise*, *ize*, and *y*

Objectives

- **Word Families:** Learn to spell words in the *ise*, *ize*, and *y* families.
- **Sight Words:** Learn to spell *liquid*, *fluid*, *weigh*, *weight*, *ounce*, *pound*, *oz.*, and *lb.* Use the sight words to complete sentences.
- **Dictionary Skills:** Match designated abbreviations with the words they stand for.
- **Endings:** Add endings to words that end in **Cy** and silent *e*.
- **Word Building:** Fill in either *ise* or *ize* to spell words in context.
- **Sound Discrimination:** Learn that /īs/ is spelled *ice* and that *ise* usually spells /īz/.
- **Writing Sentences:** Practice writing word family and sight words in context.

Sight Words

Teach the sight words using the methods described on pages 9-12 in the introduction to this book.

1 **Listening**

Introduce the words in the *ise* family using the following steps.

1. Say the sound /īz/ and ask students what letters make the sound in the first group of words.
2. Say the letters *i-s-e* and ask students what sound they make.
3. Say the word *rise* and ask students what letters spell /īz/ and what letter spells /r/.
4. Say the word *rise* and ask students what letters spell *rise*.

Follow the same steps to introduce the words in the *ize* and *y* families.

Remind students that *s* can be pronounced /s/ or /z/. Point out that *ise* and *ize* are pronounced the same.

2 **Writing Words**

Instruct students to write the words that you dictate, which are found on the replica of the student page. Say each word, use it in a phrase or simple sentence, and say the word again.

❸ Using Sight Words. Fill in the blanks in the sentences below with the sight words from this lesson. Use your dictionary if necessary.

1. (ounces, pound) There are 16 _____ounces_____ in a _____pound_____.

2. (fluid, liquid) A _____fluid_____ flows easily. A _____liquid_____ is wet.

3. (weigh, weight) To find the _____weight_____ of something you must _____weigh_____ it.

❹ Dictionary Skills: Abbreviations. Match the abbreviations below with the measurements they represent. Use your dictionary if you need to.

gal.   hr   lb.   mph   pt.
gm   kg   min   oz.   qt.

1. ounce _____oz._____   6. gram _____gm_____
2. pound _____lb._____   7. kilogram _____kg_____
3. minute _____min_____   8. pint _____pt._____
4. hour _____hr_____   9. quart _____qt._____
5. miles per hour _____mph_____   10. gallon _____gal._____

❺ Adding Endings to Words That End in Cy. When adding an ending to a word that ends in **Cy**, change the *y* to *i* unless the ending begins with *i*. Do not add *-s* to words that end in **Cy**. Instead, change the *y* to *i* and add *-es*. Add the endings above the columns to each word below. The first one has been done to get you started.

	-es	*-ed*	*-ing*
1. cry	cries	cried	crying
2. try	tries	tried	trying
3. dry	dries	dried	drying
4. deny	denies	denied	denying
5. reply	replies	replied	replying
6. supply	supplies	supplied	supplying

Lesson 17   81

❸ Using Sight Words

If students have trouble with number 2, tell them that air is fluid, but it is not liquid.

❹ Dictionary Skills: Abbreviations

Dictionaries do not always agree on whether a given abbreviation is followed by a period or not. Sometimes there is more than one abbreviation for a word as well. Tell students that any form listed in a dictionary should be considered acceptable.

❺ Adding Endings to Words That End in Cy

Before students begin this exercise, review the pattern for adding endings to words that end in **Cy**, which they learned in Lesson 14. Check to be sure they changed the *y* to *i* in the words they wrote in the first two columns, but retained the *y* in the words they wrote in the third column.

Have students pronounce the words in the **-es** column aloud. Ask them what sound each of these words ends in. Point out that the *-ies* ending is pronounced like the word families *ise* and *ize*.

6 **Review of Adding Endings.** Add the endings above the columns to each word below.

	-s or -es	-ed	-ing
1. revise	revises	revised	revising
2. apply	applies	applied	applying
3. inquire	inquires	inquired	inquiring
4. identify	identifies	identified	identifying
5. smile	smiles	smiled	smiling
6. sacrifice	sacrifices	sacrificed	sacrificing
7. rely	relies	relied	relying
8. advertise	advertises	advertised	advertising

7 **Word Building.** Words from the *ise* family are usually pronounced like the *ize* family words. Fill in the missing letters in the sentences below with either *ise* or *ize*. Use your dictionary to help you select the correct spelling if necessary.

1. Mike paid us a surpr_i_ _s_ _e_ visit last week.

2. Eileen had changed so much we hardly recogn_i_ _z_ _e_d her.

3. It is important to get plenty of good exerc_i_ _s_ _e_.

4. I real_i_ _z_ _e_ that you are busy, but we really need your help.

5. What would you adv_i_ _s_ _e_ me to do about this problem?

6. Gail apolog_i_ _z_ _e_d for not being able to come to the meeting.

7. Tonight I have to memor_i_ _z_ _e_ my lines for the play.

8. Mr. Rice is going to superv_i_ _s_ _e_ the Wednesday night craft class.

6 **Review of Adding Endings**

This exercise reviews adding endings using two different patterns:

- Silent *e* Pattern 1 (1, 3, 5, 6, and 8)
- Changing *y* to *i* in words that end in C*y* (2, 4, and 7).

Note whether students are having difficulty with either pattern, and provide additional practice as needed.

7 **Word Building**

When students have completed this exercise, review with them some of the strategies they have learned for deciding between alternative spellings for the same sound combination. These strategies include making a mental picture of the spelling of a word, developing mnemonic devices for troublesome words, selecting the most probable spelling, and looking the word up in a dictionary.

8 The Word Families *ice* and *ise*. Write each word your teacher dictates in the correct column below.

ice	*ise*
1. advice	1. advise
2. price	2. despise
3. rice	3. disguise
4. sacrifice	4. rise
5. twice	5. wise

Words in the *ise* family are usually pronounced /īz/. If you hear /īs/, it is probably spelled *ice*.

9 Writing Sentences. On the lines below, write the sentences that you hear.

1. I would advise you to take Steve's advice.
2. Amy identified the man who tried to rob her.
3. Gary's Men's Shop was advertising clothes in all sizes.
4. He will try to drain the fluid from Mike's knee.
5. Jake was in disguise so no one recognized him.
6. We have received eighteen replies to our advertisement.
7. Caroline has been trying to lose weight for a long time.
8. We were surprised when we realized our supplies were gone.
9. Mrs. Price's baby weighed seven pounds and thirteen ounces.
10. If that mixture stands awhile, the liquid will rise to the top.

8 **The Word Families *ice* and *ise***

Dictate the words on the replica of the student page in random order.

Unlike the *ace* and *ase* families and the *ise* and *ize* families, which are pronounced alike, students can hear the difference between the *ice* and *ise* families. This exercise gives them practice in hearing the differences.

9 **Writing Sentences**

Instruct students to write the sentences that you dictate, which are on the replica of the student page. Note any specific errors. Design additional sentences, words, or phrases for specific problems.

Patterns found in these sentences include:
—alternative spellings for /īz/ (1, 3, 5, 6, 8, and 10)
—possession (1, 3, 4, and 9)
—changing *y* to *i* pattern (2, 6, 7, and 8)
—Silent *e* Pattern 1 (3, 5, 6, and 8)
—adding -*s* or -*es* (3, 6, 8, 9, and 10)
—forming numbers with -*teen* (6 and 9)

Lesson 18

The Word Families *ight*, *igh*, *ign*, *ind*, and *ild*

Objectives

- **Word Families:** Learn to spell words in the *ight*, *igh*, *ign*, *ind*, and *ild* families.
- **Sight Words:** Learn to spell *altogether*, *terrible*, *usual*, *straight*, *door*, *floor*, *style*, and *type*.
- **Word Building:** Add suffixes to root words.
  Add affixes to *ign* family words.
- **Creating Sentences:** Use two *ign* words in original sentences.
- **Patterns:** Recognize and spell correctly words containing five patterns for spelling long *i*: iCe, *y*, *igh*, *ign*, and iCd.
- **Dictionary Skills:** Find the correct spelling of words containing long *i* based on phonetic spelling and meaning.
- **Writing by Syllables:** Write dictated words by syllables.
- **Sound Discrimination:** Discriminate between pairs of words that end in *ld/le* and *nd/ne*.
- **Writing Sentences:** Practice writing word family and sight words in context.

Sight Words

Teach the sight words using the methods described on pages 9-12 in the introduction to this book.

Point out that *style* and *type* are examples of other spellings for long *i*. This spelling is often referred to as the yCe spelling. Point out the silent *gh* in *straight*.

Lesson 18

The Word Families *ight*, *igh*, *ign*, *ind*, and *ild*

	Sight Words		
altogether	usual	door	style
terrible	straight	floor	type

Word Families

ight

❶ Listening

Listen to the sound *ight* makes in these words.

might	fight	night	light
sight	right	tonight	delight
tight	bright	midnight	flashlight

igh

Listen to the sound *igh* makes in these words.

high	highway	sigh	thigh

ign

Listen to the sound *ign* makes in these words.

sign	design	align
assign	resign	benign

ind

Listen to the sound *ind* makes in these words.

bind	mind	kind	blind
find	remind	kindness	behind

ild

Listen to the sound *ild* makes in these words.

child	grandchild	mild	wild

❷ Writing Words. On the lines below, write the words that you hear.

1. behind
2. sight
3. higher
4. fright
5. sighing
6. mild
7. reminder
8. flashlight
9. resign

84   Lesson 18

---

❶ Listening

Introduce the words in the *ight* family using the following steps.

1. Say the sound /īt/ and ask students what letters make the sound.
2. Say the letters *i-g-h-t* and ask students what sound they make.
3. Say the word *might* and ask students what letters spell /īt/ and what letter spells /m/.
4. Say the word *might* and ask students what letters spell *might*.

Follow the same steps to introduce the words in the *igh*, *ign*, *ind*, and *ild* families.

Point out to students that the *gh* is silent in the *igh* and *ight* patterns. Point out the silent *g* in the *ign* pattern. Tell students that words ending in *ind* or *ild* usually have a long *i*.

❷ Writing Words

Instruct students to write the words that you dictate, which are found on the replica of the student page. Say each word, use it in a phrase or simple sentence, and say the word again.

3 Word Building. Add one of the suffixes below to each word to make another form of the word.

-ed   -ing   -ish   -ly   -ness   -y

1. might ___mighty___
2. remind ___reminded___
3. mild ___mildly___
4. sigh ___sighing___
5. tight ___tightly___

6. blind ___blindness___
7. child ___childish___
8. kind ___kindness___
9. bright ___brightly___
10. fight ___fighting___

4 Word Building with *ign* Words. Add the prefixes and suffixes to the *ign* words below. Then use two of the words you formed in sentences and write the sentences on the lines at the bottom of the page. Look up their meanings in the dictionary if necessary.

1. align + ed ___aligned___
2. re + align ___realign___
3. align + ment ___alignment___
4. re + align + ment ___realignment___
5. assign + ed ___assigned___
6. un + assign + ed ___unassigned___
7. assign + ment ___assignment___
8. re + assign + ment ___reassignment___

1. _____

_____

2. _____

_____

3 Word Building

Remind students that these words end in more than one consonant and therefore endings are added without changing the root. Encourage students to use each of the endings at least once. The answers given on the replica of the student page are examples. Accept all correctly spelled words.

4 Word Building with *ign* Words

Align and *assign* lend themselves to word building with multiple affixes. The spelling of the root words does not change when the affixes are added. However, the meanings of the words are affected. Have students pronounce these words, noting the changes in meaning which the affixes create. Discuss the meanings of *re-*, *un-*, and *-ment* with students.

Additional Activity:

Write the words *sign*, *signal*, *signaled*, *signalman*, and *signature* on the board and have students pronounce them, noting the changes in syllable division and pronunciation that occur when suffixes are added to *sign*. This will heighten students' awareness of the interrelatedness of words which they might not immediately recognize as being derivatives of the same root. You might also have students use these words in sentences.

5 **Patterns for Spelling Long i.** Write the words that your teacher dictates.

1. ___time___   3. ___night___   5. ___bind___

2. ___fly___   4. ___sign___

Five different patterns that produce a long *i* sound are used in the words above. Now write one other word for each long *i* spelling pattern.

1. iCe _____   4. ign _____

2. y _____   5. iCd _____

3. igh _____

6 **Dictionary Skills: Finding the Correct Spelling.** Because there are a number of ways to spell long *i*, sometimes you won't remember which one to use. If you can't remember which spelling of long *i* to use, or if the word is new to you, check your dictionary.

Find the correct spelling of the words spelled phonetically below based on the meanings given. Write the words on the lines provided.

Phonetic Spelling	Meaning	Correct Spelling
1. /săt′ ĭs fī/	to fulfill a desire or need	satisfy
2. /rĕ vīz′/	to change or improve	revise
3. /blīnd′ fōld/	a cover for the eyes	blindfold
4. /mă līn′/	to say something harmful; to slander	malign
5. /mĕm′ə rīz/	to learn by heart	memorize
6. /blīt/	a disease that destroys plants	blight
7. /dī′ nə mīt′/	an explosive used for blasting	dynamite
8. /pīp′ līn′/	a row of tubes for carrying fluids	pipeline

86   Lesson 18

---

5 **Patterns for Spelling Long *i***

The five patterns for spelling long *i* that students have studied in this unit are reviewed in this exercise. Students must recognize that the long *i* has a number of different spellings and be ready to try a variant spelling if one spelling does not look correct.

6 **Dictionary Skills: Finding the Correct Spelling**

This exercise gives students practice in considering the alternative spellings for long *i*. Students must learn to use alternative spellings when looking up words in the dictionary. Remind them that part of the spelling process is visual monitoring and that they must ask themselves, "Does the word look right?" Encourage students to try an alternative spelling if their first attempt does not look right to them.

Additional Activity:

Have students use some or all of these words in original sentences.

7 Writing Words by Syllables. Write the words your teacher dictates by syllables. Then write the entire word. Use the syllable types to help you spell the word.

	First Syllable	Second Syllable	Third Syllable	Whole Word
1.	light	ning		lightning
2.	dis	like		dislike
3.	com	ply		comply
4.	blind	ness		blindness
5.	ex	er	cise	exercise
6.	sup	er	vise	supervise

8 Hearing Differences. Many words sound almost like other words. If they are not carefully spoken or heard, they may be misspelled. Listen carefully to the pairs of words you hear. Then write the endings in the blanks at the ends of the words.

1. mi_ld___   mi_le___   3. wi_ne___   wi_nd___
2. fi_ne___   fi_nd___   4. mi_nd___   mi_ne___

9 Writing Sentences. On the lines below, write the sentences that you hear.

1. It isn't usual for my grandchild to be so shy.
2. Don't come in the kitchen door until the floor dries.
3. I think you'll find that Dwight's child is delightful.
4. There was a terrible crash on the highway last night.
5. I have altogether too much typing to finish tonight.
6. I like the style of that dress, but the price is too high.
7. Gail makes a special kind of jelly from those berries.
8. Irene will go straight to work when she finishes the assignment.

Lesson 18   87

7 Writing Words by Syllables

Dictate each word by syllables, emphasizing the syllables. Then pronounce the whole word normally. Remind students that the number of blanks indicates the number of syllables in the word.

Note any particular patterns with which students are having difficulty. You might ask them to check any words they are uncertain of in the dictionary.

Additional Activities:

Have students identify the types of syllables they have written by using C for closed, O for open, VCe, Cle, or D for double vowel syllables.

Have students look up the meanings of any of these words that they don't already know.

Have them use some of the words in original sentences.

8 Hearing Differences

Sometimes students misspell words because they are spelling words according to an incorrect pronunciation. This exercise contrasts iCe words with iCd words.

Be sure to pronounce the second word in number 3 as /wīnd/, not as /wĭnd/.

9 Writing Sentences

Instruct students to write the sentences that you dictate, which are on the replica of the student page. Note any specific errors. Design additional sentences, words, or phrases for specific problems.

Patterns found in these sentences include:
—contractions (1, 2, and 3)
—changing *y* to *i* pattern (2 and 7)
—possession (3)
—adding prefixes and suffixes (3 and 8)
—double consonants in the middle of words (4, 7, and 8)
—Silent *e* Pattern 1 (5)
—adding -*s* or -*es* (7 and 8)

Review of Unit 3
The Long *i*

Objectives

- **Word Building:** Add iCe families to initial consonants, blends, and digraphs.
- **Patterns:** Review alternative ways of spelling long *i*.
- **Familiar Sayings:** Fill in long *i* words to complete familiar sayings.
- **Endings:** Review six patterns for adding endings.
  Identify root words and the patterns followed to form specific words.
  Add endings to words following the six patterns.
- **Syllable Types:** Review five types of syllables.
- **Writing by Syllables:** Write dictated words by syllables.
- **Irregular Verbs:** Use irregular forms of designated verbs to complete sentences.
- **Creating Sentences:** Write an original story using word family and sight words.
- **Writing Sentences:** Practice writing word family and sight words in context.
- **Puzzle:** Review long *i* family words and sight words by completing a crossword puzzle.

❶ Word Building with iCe Families

Have students add one of the iCe word families to each consonant, blend, or digraph to make a word. Since there are more families than there are consonants, they will not be able to use all of the families. Encourage them to use as many as possible. The answers given on the replica of the student page are examples. Accept all correctly spelled words.

Review of Unit 3
The Long *i*

❶ Word Building with iCe Families. Add one of the word families listed below to each of the consonants or blends to make a word.

ime	ike	ipe	ine	ide	ife	ise
ibe	ice	ile	ire	ite	ive	ize

1. b _ike_
2. d _ime_
3. h _ire_
4. l _ine_
5. m _ile_
6. p _ipe_
7. s _ide_
8. w _ife_
9. br _ibe_
10. pr _ize_
11. tw _ice_
12. wh _ite_

❷ Other Patterns for Spelling Long *i*. One pattern that produces long *i* is iCe. Four other patterns that you learned in Unit 3 are listed below. Write three words for each pattern.

1. igh _____ _____ _____
2. ign _____ _____ _____
3. y _____ _____ _____
4. iCd _____ _____ _____

❸ Familiar Sayings. Fill in the blanks in these familiar sayings with the long *i* words below.

bride	eyes	kite	shines	time
divided	fly	nine	sight	united

1. Go _fly_ a _kite_.
2. A stitch in _time_ saves _nine_.
3. Happy is the _bride_ that the sun _shines_ on.
4. _United_ we stand, _divided_ we fall.
5. You are a _sight_ for sore _eyes_.

88   Review of Unit 3

---

❷ Other Patterns for Spelling Long *i*

This exercise reviews the four other spellings for long *i* that students learned in this unit. Remind them that long *i* at the end of a word is usually spelled *y*. You might also remind them that the yCe pattern exists but is uncommon. The sight words *rhyme*, *style*, and *type* follow this pattern.

❸ Familiar Sayings

When students have completed this exercise, discuss the meanings of the various sayings.

Additional Activity:

Have students think of other sayings that have long *i* words in them.

❹ Reviewing Patterns for Endings

This exercise reviews the major patterns for adding endings that students have learned so far. Patterns 2 and 4 were covered in Book 1 of this series. If any of your students have started in Book 2, you will want to pre-teach these two patterns.

Removing the ending to find the root word draws students' attention to the spelling changes which have occurred in many of the words.

5 **Adding Endings.** Add the designated endings to each of the words below.

1. rely + ing   _relying_   11. light + ly   _lightly_
2. dine + er   _diner_   12. tap + ed   _tapped_
3. life + s or es   _lives_   13. greedy + er   _greedier_
4. big + er   _bigger_   14. try + al   _trial_
5. bike + ing   _biking_   15. kidney + s or es   _kidneys_
6. fix + s or es   _fixes_   16. beach + s or es   _beaches_
7. sew + ing   _sewing_   17. rid + ing   _ridding_
8. deny + al   _denial_   18. ride + ing   _riding_
9. reply + s or es   _replies_   19. leaf + s or es   _leaves_
10. speech + s or es   _speeches_   20. invite + ed   _invited_

6 **Reviewing Syllable Types**

1. Circle each closed syllable below.

(con) (bin) o vite (fun) bo tle bock teem (ip)

2. Circle each open syllable below.

(bo) in (o) vite (be) tle cape (la) tain (ra)

3. Circle each Cle syllable below.

bo in o vite (tle) hap il (ble) re i

4. Circle each VCe syllable below.

(cate) in o (vite) tle hap il (cape) ceal re

5. Circle each double vowel syllable below.

cate in (ceed) vite tle (beat) (tain) ble (ceal) hap

5 **Adding Endings**

This exercise also reviews the six patterns for adding endings learned so far. Note any patterns with which students are having trouble, and plan reinforcement exercises as needed.

6 **Reviewing Syllable Types**

This exercise reviews the five syllable types students have studied. Review the attributes of each syllable type before students begin this exercise.

7 Writing Words by Syllables. Write the words your teacher dictates by syllables. Then write the entire word on the line provided.

	First Syllable	Second Syllable	Third Syllable	Fourth Syllable	Whole Word
1.	i	o	dine		iodine
2.	rec	on	cile		reconcile
3.	de	light	ful		delightful
4.	e	con	o	mize	economize
5.	so	ci	e	ty	society
6.	i	den	ti	fy	identify

Challenge word:

i	tin	er	ar	y	itinerary

8 Using Irregular Verbs. Fill in the blanks in the sentences below with the correct form of the verb in parentheses. Look up the verbs in your dictionary if necessary.

1. (find)   Have you __found__ your notebook yet?

2. (slide)   The batter __slid__ into second base and was safe.

3. (ride)   Have you ever __ridden__ on a trolley?

4. (rise)   I was awake before the sun __rose__ this morning.

5. (fight)   The committee has __fought__ hard to get the plans accepted.

6. (bind)   Dwight has __bound__ the crates with good, strong rope.

7. (write)   I have __written__ them several letters, but they haven't responded.

8. (rise)   The number of graduates has __risen__ sharply over the past five years.

7 Writing Words by Syllables

Dictate each word by syllables, emphasizing the syllables. Then pronounce the whole word normally. Remind students that the number of blanks indicates the number of syllables in the word.

The word *identify* includes an open syllable with a short vowel (*ti*). Point out that knowing syllable types and their characteristics is useful, but not every syllable is true to the patterns they have learned. A medial syllable including an *i* is especially prone to other pronun- ciations, in this case short *i*. Point out that a syllable with an *i* that comes in the middle of a word is often pronounced with a short *i*.

8 Using Irregular Verbs

These are all verbs from Unit 3 word families that have irregular principal parts. Encourage students to use their dictionaries to look up the principal parts if they need to. If they are keeping a table of irregular verbs in their notebooks, have them add these to the list.

9 **Creating Sentences**. On a separate sheet of paper, write a story about the three pictures below. Use some of the following long *i* words from Unit 3.

night	fright	shine	recognize	reply
time	while	flashlight	sight	criticize
tired	try	surprise	why	apologize
wife	excited	identify	remind	sacrifice

2 a.m.

Moments later

Still later

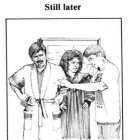

10 **Writing Sentences**. On the lines below, write the sentences that you hear.

1. Irene found the knives that were missing from that set.
2. Can you find five words that rhyme with *type*?
3. I'm trying to economize by riding my bike to work.
4. Have you decided on an itinerary for your journey?
5. Dwight designed a fine high chair for my grandchild.
6. They didn't assign us enough supplies to do the job right.
7. Mike saw a bright light shining when he drove by at midnight.
8. Both boxes were filled with papers, so I did some filing.

92   Review of Unit 3

9 Creating Sentences

Discuss the pictures with students before they begin to write so that they can get some ideas for their stories.

You may wish to talk to them about tone and style. Do they want to be serious? Melodramatic? Allow students to enjoy this exercise.

Encourage them to use as many long *i* and sight words as they can. Be concerned about words and patterns already studied, but do not worry too much about other words.

10 Writing Sentences

Instruct students to write the sentences that you dictate, which are on the replica of the student page. Note any specific errors. Design additional sentences, words, or phrases for specific problems.

Patterns found in these sentences include:

—changing *f* or *fe* to *v* (1)
—adding *-s* or *-es* (1, 2, 6, and 8)
—irregular verb forms (1 and 7)
—Silent *e* Pattern 1 (3, 4, 7, and 8)
—changing *y* to *i* pattern (6)
—contractions (3 and 6)
—polysyllabic words (4)

11 **Crossword Puzzle.** Use the clues below to complete the puzzle. Most of the answers are word family and sight words from Unit 3.

Across

1. Get up
3. Measured the weight of something
6. This connects your arm to your body.
10. When two words end in the same sound they do this.
11. The opposite of answer
13. May: I ____ go shopping tonight.
14. Gentle: A ____ breeze blew.
16. To operate a car
17. The person who steers the car
18. Made up your mind: Have you ____ to go with us?

Down

1. Reply
2. A long, drawn-out breath
3. The opposite of tame
4. ____ and seek
5. A plan or pattern used for making something
6. Where the clouds are
7. Beyond the regular hours
8. Not a solid or gas; something wet
9. What you do to stay fit
12. What the clock tells
13. You use this to think.
15. Changed the color: She ____ her rug blue.

Review of Unit 3   93

11 **Crossword Puzzle**

Encourage students to look at the puzzle blanks to enable them to use word length as an additional clue. If needed, supply students with the following list of answer words. Tell them to cross off words as they use them.

answer	mild
arise	mind
decided	overtime
design	question
drive	rhyme
driver	shoulder
dyed	sigh
exercise	sky
hide	time
liquid	weighed
might	wild

Unit 3 Tests

We recommend that you test your students on the word family and sight words from Unit 3 before going on. The following are suggested lists of representative family words and sight words from Unit 3. You may want to substitute other words to meet the needs of your students.

Dictate each word and use it in a simple sentence. Students should be able to spell 90 percent of these words correctly.

Family Words	Sight Words
1. mine	1. type
2. life	2. cough
3. nice	3. door
4. prize	4. ounce
5. wipe	5. group
6. sight	6. question
7. child	7. liquid
8. pride	8. court
9. high	9. straight
10. alike	10. pound
11. unite	11. weight
12. supply	12. both
13. revise	13. usual
14. inquire	14. route
15. driveway	15. answer
16. sometimes	16. shoulder
17. meanwhile	17. altogether
18. describe	18. thorough
19. kindness	19. rhyme
20. design	20. terrible

Lesson 19

The Word Families *ope*, *one*, *oke*, *ome*, and *ove*

Objectives

- **Word Families:** Learn to spell words in the *ope*, *one*, *oke*, *ome*, and *ove* families.
- **Sight Words:** Learn to spell *most, almost, ready, already, always,* and *all right*.
  Use the sight words to complete sentences.
- **Word Building:** Add word families to initial consonants and blends.
- **Syllable Types:** Write words that contain **VCe** syllables.
  Review five types of syllables by categorizing examples.
- **Pattern:** Add endings to words that end in silent *e*.
- **Writing by Syllables:** Write dictated words by syllables.
- **Writing Sentences:** Practice writing word family and sight words in context.

Sight Words

Teach the sight words using the methods described on pages 9-12 in the introduction to this book. Contrast *almost, already,* and *always* with *all right*. Tell students that *all right* is always spelled as two words.

Lesson 19

The Word Families *ope*, *one*, *oke*, *ome*, and *ove*

Sight Words		
most	ready	always
almost	already	all right

Word Families	
ope	**1** Listening
	Listen to the sound *ope* makes in these words.
	hope rope envelope
	cope slope telescope
one	Listen to the sound *one* makes in these words.
	bone phone lone shone
	tone telephone alone stone
	zone postpone lonely
oke	Listen to the sound *oke* makes in these words.
	joke smoke broke revoke
	poke spoke broken provoke
	woke stroke
ome	Listen to the sound *ome* makes in these words.
	dome homeless Nome
	home homesick Rome
ove	Listen to the sound *ove* makes in these words.
	cove rove grove stove
	drove wove strove stovepipe

94   Lesson 19

---

1 **Listening**

Introduce the words in the *ope* family using the following steps.

1. Say the sound /ōp/ and ask students what letters make the sound.
2. Say the letters *o-p-e* and ask students what sound they make.
3. Say the word *hope* and ask students what letters spell /ōp/ and what letter spells /h/.
4. Say the word *hope* and ask students what letters spell *hope*.

Follow the same steps to introduce the words in the *one, oke, ome,* and *ove* families.

Point out that the *one* family is spelled like the number *one* but is pronounced differently.

When you have introduced the *ove* family words, ask students if they can remember any sight words that end in *ove* but are pronounced differently. They may recall *love* (Lesson 10 in Book 1), *move,* and *prove* (Lesson 7 in this book). Explain that they are sight words because they are pronounced differently from the *ove* family words.

2 **Writing Words.** On the lines below, write the words that you hear.

1. bones   4. phoning   7. stoves

2. hoping   5. choke   8. broken

3. woven   6. homesick   9. envelope

3 **Word Building.** Add either *ope*, *one*, *oke*, *ome*, or *ove* to each of the consonants to make a word. Do not make the same word twice.

1. c one   4. j oke   7. dr ove

2. h ope   5. r ove   8. gr ope

3. h ome   6. t one   9. st one

4 **Using Sight Words.** Fill in the blanks in the sentences below with the sight words from this lesson. Use each word only once.

1. A square always has four sides of equal length.

2. The Earth is almost a perfect sphere.

3. China is the most populous country on Earth.

4. Firemen must be ready to respond at a moment's notice.

5. Many scientists believe the greenhouse effect has already begun.

6. It is all right to plant seedlings when there is no more danger of frost.

5 **The VCe Syllable Type.** As you know, a **VCe** syllable ends in a silent *e*. This silent *e* usually causes the vowel to be long. For each of the vowels below, write three words that follow the **VCe** pattern and contain the long vowel sound.

1. a _____   _____   _____

2. e _____   _____   _____

3. i _____   _____   _____

4. o _____   _____   _____

Lesson 19   95

2 Writing Words

Instruct students to write the words that you dictate, which are found on the replica of the student page. Say each word, use it in a phrase or simple sentence, and say the word again.

3 Word Building

Have students add one of the word families to each consonant or blend to make a word. Encourage them to use all of the word families at least once. The answers given on the replica of the student page are examples. Accept all correctly spelled words.

4 Using Sight Words

This exercise gives students an opportunity to use the sight words in context. Stress the differences in usage between *most* and *almost* and between *ready* and *already*. Remind students that *all right* is always two words.

5 The VCe Syllable Type

If students have trouble remembering three eCe words, refer them to Exercise 4 in Lesson 13. If they have trouble with the oCe words, point out that all the families in this lesson are of this type.

6 **Review of Silent _e_ Pattern 1.** The silent _e_ at the end of a word is dropped when an ending starting with a vowel is added. The silent _e_ is not dropped when the ending starts with a consonant. Add the endings to the words below and write the new words on the lines provided.

1. cope + ed ____coped____
2. zone + ing ____zoning____
3. hope + ful ____hopeful____
4. joke + er ____joker____
5. dome + ed ____domed____

6. spoke + en ____spoken____
7. smoke + er ____smoker____
8. phone + ing ____phoning____
9. bone + less ____boneless____
10. broke + er ____broker____

7 **Reviewing Syllable Types.** Write each syllable below on a line under the correct heading.

reel	gle	so	muf	kle
gal	ment	re	e	voke
tail	ade	tle	nate	aim
pro	tract	file	cle	veal

Closed
1. ____gal____
2. ____ment____
3. ____tract____
4. ____muf____

Open
1. ____pro____
2. ____so____
3. ____re____
4. ____e____

Cle
1. ____gle____
2. ____tle____
3. ____cle____
4. ____kle____

VCe
1. ____ade____
2. ____file____
3. ____nate____
4. ____voke____

Double
1. ____reel____
2. ____tail____
3. ____aim____
4. ____veal____

6 **Review of Silent _e_ Pattern 1**

Note if any students are still having trouble with this pattern. Design reinforcement activities as needed.

7 **Reviewing Syllable Types**

Review the attributes of the five syllable types before students begin this exercise.

8 **Writing Words by Syllables.** Write the words that you hear one syllable at a time. Then write the whole word on the line at the right. Use the syllable types to help you spell the word.

	First Syllable	Second Syllable	Third Syllable	Whole Word
1.	top	ple		topple
2.	re	store		restore
3.	pro	pose		propose
4.	ca	pa	ble	capable
5.	ex	cit	ed	excited
6.	home	sick	ness	homesickness
7.	com	pla	cent	complacent
8.	e	lope	ment	elopement

9 **Writing Sentences.** On the lines below, write the sentences that you hear.

1. I am almost always ready to go home by five o'clock
2. Bing Crosby used to sing a song called "High Hopes."
3. The fire was still smoking when we arrived at the grove.
4. Almost everyone had already heard about their elopement.
5. Many cities are having trouble coping with homeless people.
6. Most of the time, Grover is ready for work by eight o'clock.
7. Hope had already spoken to me about postponing the meeting.

8. Is it all right to telephone your home after eleven o'clock?

8 **Writing Words by Syllables**

Dictate each word by syllables, emphasizing the syllables. Then pronounce the whole word normally. Remind students that the number of blanks indicates the number of syllables in the word.

Point out that number 4, *capable*, contains an open syllable with a short vowel (*pa*). Remind students that these are sometimes found in the middle of words.

Additional Activities:

Have students look up the meanings of any of these words, such as *complacent*, that they don't already know.

Have them use some of the words in original sentences.

9 **Writing Sentences**

Instruct students to write the sentences that you dictate, which are on the replica of the student page. Note any specific errors. Design additional sentences, words, or phrases for specific problems.

Sentence 2 has a song title in it. You may want to review capitalization and punctuation of titles before beginning the dictation.

Watch for students having trouble with the sight words beginning with *al*. Common misspellings include misspelling *all right* as *alright* and *already* as *allready* or *all ready*.

Patterns found in these sentences include:
—Silent *e* Pattern 1 (2, 3, 4, 5, and 7)
—adding -*s* or -*es* (2 and 5)
—irregular verb forms (4 and 7)
—changing *y* to *i* pattern (5)

Lesson 20
The Word Families *obe*, *ote*, *ode*, *ore*, *ose*, and *oze*

Objectives

- **Word Families:** Learn to spell words in the *obe, ote, ode, ore, ose,* and *oze* families.
- **Sight Words:** Learn to spell *woman*, *women*, *hurry*, *worry*, *spouse*, and *husband*.
- **Word Building:** Fill in either *ose* or *oze* to spell words in context.
- **Root Words:** Identify roots in words with affixes.
- **Endings:** Add endings to designated words.
- **Creating Sentences:** Use words with affixes in original sentences.
- **Using Words in Context:** Complete paragraphs by filling in word family and sight words.
- **Writing Sentences:** Practice writing word family and sight words in context.

Sight Words

Teach the sight words using the methods described on pages 9-12 in the introduction to this book. Note that when forming the plural of *woman*, the spelling of the first syllable remains the same even though the pronunciation changes. Point out that although *hurry* and *worry* rhyme they are spelled with different vowels.

Lesson 20
The Word Families *obe*, *ote*, *ode*, *ore*, *ose*, and *oze*

Sight Words		
woman	hurry	spouse
women	worry	husband

Word Families

❶ Listening

obe

Listen to the sound *obe* makes in these words.

robe	lobe	strobe
probe	globe	

ote

Listen to the sound *ote* makes in these words.

note	vote	quote	devote
notebook	voter	wrote	remote

ode

Listen to the sound *ode* makes in these words.

code	mode	erode
zip code	rode	explode

ore

Listen to the sound *ore* makes in these words.

ore	tore	chore	before
core	store	shore	folklore
sore	restore	shoreline	moreover

ose

Listen to the sound *ose* makes in these words.

hose	pose	close	chose
nose	expose	disclose	those
rose	suppose		

oze

Listen to the sound *oze* makes in these words.

doze	bulldozer	froze	frozen

---

❶ Listening

Introduce the words in the *obe* family using the following steps.

1. Say the sound /ōb/ and ask students what letters make the sound.
2. Say the letters *o-b-e* and ask students what sound they make.
3. Say the word *robe* and ask students what letters spell /ōb/ and what letter spells /r/.
4. Say the word *robe* and ask students what letters spell *robe*.

Follow the same steps to introduce the words in the *ote, ode, ore, ose,* and *oze* families.

Point out the silent *w* in *wrote* and the silent *l* in *folklore*.

Point out that both *ose* and *oze* are pronounced /ōz/. Note that *close* can be pronounced both /klōs/ and /klōz/, depending on its meaning in context.

2 **Writing Words.** On the lines below, write the words that you hear.

1. tore
2. code
3. noted
4. chose
5. wore
6. robe
7. wrote
8. rode
9. rose
10. froze
11. disclosing
12. before

3 **Word Building.** Many words from the *ose* family are pronounced like the *oze* family words. Fill in the missing letters in the sentences below with either *ose* or *oze*.

1. We left the h o s e outside and it fr o z e.
2. R o s e wanted to stay awake for the late show, but she d o z e d off.
3. I supp o s e you ch o s e that tie to go with your shirt.
4. Th o s e flowers were exp o s e d to the cold and were fr o z e n.
5. Mike drove the bulld o z e r right through the r o s e bushes.

4 **Finding Root Words.** Write the root word for each of the words below on the lines provided.

1. hopeful — hope
2. denote — note
3. compose — pose
4. telephone — phone
5. homeless — home
6. exposure — pose *or* expose
7. voter — vote
8. lonely — lone
9. rewrote — wrote
10. disclose — close
11. remotely — remote
12. telescope — scope
13. notable — note
14. global — globe

Lesson 20   99

---

2 **Writing Words**

Instruct students to write the words that you dictate, which are found on the replica of the student page. Say each word, use it in a phrase or simple sentence, and say the word again.

3 **Word Building**

When students have completed this exercise, review with them some of the strategies they have learned for deciding between alternative spellings for the same sound combination. These strategies include creating a mental picture of the spelling of a word, developing mnemonic devices for troublesome words, selecting the most probable spelling, and using the dictionary. Point out that since there are more words in the *ose* family, this spelling is more probable than *oze*.

4 **Finding Root Words**

The words in this exercise contain both prefixes and suffixes. Point this out to students before they begin. If students have trouble finding the root words for numbers 6, 13, and 14, have them review Silent *e* Pattern 1.

❺ Adding Endings. Add the endings to each of the words below and write the new words on the lines provided.

1. joke + ing   joking
2. robe + ed   robed
3. rob + ed   robbed
4. store + age   storage
5. quote + able   quotable
6. snore + ed   snored
7. globe + al   global
8. hope + ing   hoping
9. hop + ing   hopping
10. erode + ing   eroding

11. remote + ly   remotely
12. jersey + s or es   jerseys
13. probe + ing   probing
14. deny + s or es   denies
15. teach + s or es   teaches
16. disclose + ed   disclosed
17. wolf + s or es   wolves
18. lone + ly + ness   loneliness
19. suppose + ed + ly   supposedly
20. hope + less + ly   hopelessly

❻ Creating Sentences. Choose five of the words you wrote in Exercise 5 and use them in sentences.

1. _____
_____
2. _____
_____
3. _____
_____
4. _____
_____
5. _____
_____

100   Lesson 20

❺ Adding Endings

This exercise reviews all the patterns for adding endings that were listed in Exercise 4 of the Review of Unit 3. You may want to review these patterns before students begin this exercise. Note any patterns that students are having trouble with. Pay particular attention to numbers 2 and 3 and numbers 8 and 9, in which Silent *e* Pattern 1 is contrasted with Doubling Pattern 1. Also, check to be sure students change the *y* to *i* before adding *ness* in number 18.

❻ Creating Sentences

Encourage students to use as many of these words as they can in their sentences.

If students ask how to spell a word that they have not studied, encourage them to look it up in the dictionary. Remember that errors in words that haven't been studied shouldn't be treated negatively. Point out any parts of the word that are spelled correctly and praise the effort.

7 **Using Words.** Fill in the blanks in the story with the words listed below. Use each word only once.

arose	exposed	spoke	voters
bulldozer	hurry	those	worried
chose	ignored	voted	wrote

Many people __voted__ in the local elections last week. They __chose__ a new mayor and three new members of the town council.

Eight months ago, a problem __arose__. Toxic waste was __exposed__ when a __bulldozer__ uncovered an old dump site. This __worried__ many people. They wanted the toxic waste cleaned up in a __hurry__. Many people __wrote__ letters to the editor of the newspaper and __spoke__ out at town council meetings.

But the mayor and several councilors __ignored__ their demands. Last week, the __voters__ turned __those__ officials out of office when they went to the polls.

8 **Writing Sentences.** On the lines below, write the sentences that you hear.

1. That woman's husband operates a bulldozer.
2. Many forms ask for the name of your spouse.
3. Please close the door after you put your clothes away.
4. Four of the women hurried to the store before it closed.
5. The rocket carried a probe which will explore nearby planets.
6. Even in the most remote places on the globe, ideas are changing.
7. Those people are worried that the shoreline will erode even more.
8. Rosemary is devoting most of her time to caring for the homeless.

7 **Using Words**

This exercise gives students a chance to see and use their word family and sight words in context. Suggest that students check off each word as they use it, so that the process of elimination will help them find the answers. When they have filled in all the answers, have them read the entire story for comprehension.

8 **Writing Sentences**

Instruct students to write the sentences that you dictate, which are on the replica of the student page. Note any specific errors. Design additional sentences, words, or phrases for specific problems.

Patterns found in these sentences include:
—alternative spellings for /ōz/ (1, 3, 4, 7, and 8)
—Silent *e* Pattern 1 (1, 4, 6, and 8)
—adding -*s* or -*es* (1, 2, 5, and 6)
—possession (1)
—changing *y* to *i* pattern (4, 5, and 7)

Lesson 21
The Word Families *ole*, *oll*, *old*, and *olt*

Objectives

- **Word Families**: Learn to spell words in the *ole*, *oll*, *old*, and *olt* families.
- **Sight Words:** Learn to spell *during*, *skiing*, *moth*, *cloth*, *canoe*, *promise*, *soul*, and *spirit*.
- **Dictionary Skills:** Use the dictionary to find the correct spelling of words that end in /ōl/.
  Learn to discriminate between homonyms that end in /ōl/. Find irregular forms of designated verbs.
- **Word Building:** Add *old*, *oled*, or *olled* to build words in context.
- **Syllable Types:** Review five types of syllables.
- **Writing by Syllables:** Write dictated words by syllables.
- **Writing Sentences:** Practice writing word family and sight words in context.

Sight Words

Teach the sight words using the methods described on pages 9-12 in the introduction to this book. Point out the *ou* spelling for the long *o* in *soul*.

❶ Listening

Introduce the words in the *ole* family using the following steps.

1. Say the sound /ōl/ and ask students what letters make the sound.
2. Say the letters *o-l-e* and ask students what sound they make.
3. Say the word *mole* and ask students what letters spell /ōl/ and what letter spells /m/.
4. Say the word *mole* and ask students what letters spell *mole*.

Lesson 21
The Word Families *ole*, *oll*, *old*, and *olt*

Sight Words			
during	moth	canoe	soul
skiing	cloth	promise	spirit

Word Families

ole

❶ Listening

Listen to the sound *ole* makes in these words.

mole	sole	whole	hole
pole	stole	wholesome	keyhole
role	parole	wholesale	buttonhole

oll

Listen to the sound *oll* makes in these words.

roll	poll	stroll	knoll
enroll	toll	swollen	wholly

old

Listen to the sound *old* makes in these words.

hold	bold	golden
sold	cold	withhold
told	scold	blindfold

olt

Listen to the sound *olt* makes in these words.

colt	bolt	revolt
jolted	voltage	

❷ Writing Words. On the lines below, write the words that you hear.

1. hole
2. toll
3. jolted
4. sold
5. fold
6. enroll
7. whole
8. wholly
9. stolen
10. revolting
11. paroled
12. withhold

When you introduce the word *sole*, point out that it is a homonym of the sight word *soul*.

Follow the same steps to introduce the words in the *oll*, *old*, and *olt* families.

Point out that syllables ending in olC, such as *oll*, *old*, and *olt*, often produce the long *o* sound.

Point out the silent *w* in *whole*, *wholesome*, and *wholesale*. Point out the silent *w* in *wholly* and note that the *e* has been dropped before adding *ly*, which is an exception to the regular pattern.

❷ Writing Words

Instruct students to write the words that you dictate, which are found on the replica of the student page. Say each word, use it in a phrase or simple sentence, and say the word again.

Watch for homonym misspellings with words such as *hole* (number 1) and *whole* (number 7). It is important to clear up homonym spelling confusions as early as possible so they won't become "cemented" in a student's writing. Note also if students spelled *paroled* correctly. If not, review Silent *e* Pattern 1 with them.

3 **Dictionary Skills: Finding the Correct Spelling.** There are two common spellings for /ōl/: *oll* and *ole*. Use the dictionary to find the correct spelling for the words below based on the meanings given. When you find the spelling that matches the meaning, write the word in the appropriate column.

Phonetic Spelling	Meaning	oll	ole
1. /bōl/	a seedpod of the cotton plant	boll	
2. /dōl/	to give out small portions		dole
3. /drōl/	amusing, comical	droll	
4. /tăd´pōl/	a young frog or toad		tadpole
5. /skrōl/	a roll of writing material	scroll	
6. /loop´hōl/	a way to avoid or evade something		loophole

4 **Dictionary Skills: Homonyms.** Answer the following questions using your dictionary if necessary.

1. Does a doughnut have a *hole* or a *whole*? _____hole_____

2. Was the flag on top of the *pole* or the *poll*? _____pole_____

3. Did the car *role* or *roll* down the hill? _____roll_____

4. Is the spirit of something a *sole* or a *soul*? _____soul_____

5 **Word Building.** Words in the *old* family sound like the past tense of words in the *oll* and *ole* families. Fill in the blanks in the sentences below with *old*, *oled*, or *olled*. Use your dictionary to check any spellings you are not sure of.

1. Are you enr_olled_ in any courses this semester?

2. That bread has m_old_ on it.

3. Dora str_olled_ along the deserted beach.

4. I asked Norman to f_old_ his clothes neatly.

5. When Ryan broke his leg, we cons_oled_ him with a gallon of ice cream.

Lesson 21   103

---

3 Dictionary Skills: Finding the Correct Spelling

Unlike previous exercises of this type, none of the words included here are in the listening exercise, so students will probably have to look them all up in the dictionary. When students have successfully listed the words in the correct columns, discuss with them the strategies that will help them remember how to spell these words.

4 Dictionary Skills: Homonyms

When students have finished this exercise, discuss the meaning of the other homonym in each pair. Be sure students know the meaning of both homonyms in each pair.

5 Word Building

Note any of these forms with which students have trouble. If necessary, develop additional sentences to give students practice in correctly spelling words that end in /ōld/.

6 **Dictionary Skills: Irregular Verbs.** Look up the following verbs in the dictionary, and write the different forms in the appropriate columns.

Present Tense	Past Tense	Have, Has, or Had + Verb	-ing Form of Verb
1. sell	sold	sold	selling
2. speak	spoke	spoken	speaking
3. hold	held	held	holding
4. choose	chose	chosen	choosing
5. tell	told	told	telling
6. break	broke	broken	breaking
7. swell	swelled	swelled *or* swollen	swelling
8. freeze	froze	frozen	freezing
9. shine	shone *or* shined	shone *or* shined	shining
10. wear	wore	worn	wearing

7 **Syllable Types.** The five types of syllables you have studied so far are listed below. An example of each type is given. Write another example of each type of syllable on the lines provided.

Syllable Type	Example	Your Example
1. Closed	hot	_____
2. Open	so	_____
3. Cle	ple	_____
4. VCe	ope	_____
5. Double Vowel	oat	_____

6 **Dictionary Skills: Irregular Verbs**

Review the principal parts of verbs before students begin this exercise. If students are keeping a table of irregular verbs in their notebooks, have them add these to the list. Accept either form of the past participles of *swell* and *shine*.

7 **Syllable Types**

Review the attributes of each type of syllable before students begin this exercise. Accept all correct responses.

8 **Writing Words by Syllables.** Write the words your teacher dictates by syllables. Then write the entire word on the line provided.

	First Syllable	Second Syllable	Third Syllable	Fourth Syllable	Whole Word
1.	e	lec	trode		electrode
2.	note	wor	thy		noteworthy
3.	pro	pos	al		proposal
4.	with	hold	ing		withholding
5.	ep	i	sode		episode
6.	o	be	di	ent	obedient
7.	dis	pos	a	ble	disposable
8.	O	ri	en	tal	Oriental

Challenge word:

e lec tro car di o gram   electrocardiogram

9 **Writing Sentences.** On the lines below, write the sentences that you hear.

1. Gail goes skiing every weekend during the winter.
2. Didn't I tell you that Rose sold her canoe to Grover?
3. The salesperson rolled out a bolt of golden cloth.
4. Broken promises make voters lose faith in their leaders.
5. Rosemary put her heart and soul into playing that role.
6. Moths will make holes in that cloth if you're not careful.
7. Their team spirit was high after their losing streak was broken.
8. Children sometimes are told not to speak until they are spoken to.

8 **Writing Words by Syllables**

Dictate each word by syllables, emphasizing the syllables. Then pronounce the whole word normally. Remind students that the number of blanks indicates the number of syllables in the word.

Number 8, *Oriental*, is often capitalized. You may wish to point this out to students.

Additional Activities:

Have students look up the meanings of any of these words that they don't already know.

Have them use some of the words in original sentences.

9 **Writing Sentences**

Instruct students to write the sentences that you dictate, which are on the replica of the student page. Note any specific errors. Design additional sentences, words, or phrases for specific problems.

Patterns found in these sentences include:
—alternative spellings for /ōld/ (2, 3, and 8)
—irregular verb forms (2, 4, 7, and 8)
—contractions (2 and 6)
—adding -*s* and -*es* (4 and 6)
—alternative spellings for /ōl/ (5 and 6)
—Silent *e* Pattern 1 (6 and 7)

Lesson 22
The Word Families *oat*, *oam*, *oal*, *oad*, *oan*, *oak*, *oast*, and *oach*

Objectives

- **Word Families:** Learn to spell words in the *oat*, *oam*, *oal*, *oad*, *oan*, *oak*, *oast*, and *oach* families.
- **Sight Words:** Learn to spell *inch*, *centimeter*, *foot*, *meter*, *yard* and *kilometer*.
  Use the sight words to complete sentences.
- **Pattern:** Discover that *oa* is an alternative spelling for long *o*.
- **Dictionary Skills:** Find abbreviations for common units of measure.
  Use the dictionary to spell homonyms correctly.
- **Sound Discrimination:** Learn to discriminate between pairs of words that sound similar.
- **Creating Sentences:** Write an original story using word family and sight words.
- **Writing Sentences:** Practice writing word family and sight words in context.

Sight Words

Teach the sight words using the methods described on pages 9-12 in the introduction to this book.

❶ Listening

Introduce the words in the *oat* family using the following steps.

1. Say the sound /ōt/ and ask students what letters make the sound.

2. Say the letters *o-a-t* and ask students what sound they make.
3. Say the word *oats* and ask students what letters spell /ōt/ and what letter spells /s/.
4. Say the word *oats* and ask students what letters spell *oats*.

Follow the same steps to introduce the words in the *oam*, *oal*, *oad*, *oan*, *oak*, *oast*, and *oach* families.

Additional Activities:

The representative family words in this lesson present a good opportunity to review compound words. Have students tell you what two words make up *overcoat*, *sailboat*, *carload*, *railroad*, *coastline*, *stagecoach*, and *cockroach*. Contrast these closed compounds with the open compounds *field goal* and *roller coaster*.

Ask students if they can think of other compound words using these word families. Have them use their dictionaries to see if they are open, closed, or hyphenated compounds.

Lesson 22
The Word Families *oat*, *oam*, *oal*, *oad*, *oan*, *oak*, *oast*, and *oach*

Sight Words		
inch	foot	yard
centimeter	meter	kilometer

Word Families	
	❶ Listening
oat	Listen to the sound *oat* makes in these words.
	oats · coat · boat · gloat · float · overcoat · sailboat · throat
oam	Listen to the sound *oam* makes in these words.
	foam · roam · styrofoam
oal	Listen to the sound *oal* makes in these words.
	coal · charcoal · goal · field goal
oad	Listen to the sound *oad* makes in these words.
	load · road · goad · carload · railroad · toad
oan	Listen to the sound *oan* makes in these words.
	Joan · loan · moan · groan
oak	Listen to the sound *oak* makes in these words.
	oak · cloak · croak · soak
oast	Listen to the sound *oast* makes in these words.
	boast · roast · coastal · coaster · coast · toast · coastline · roller coaster
oach	Listen to the sound *oach* makes in these words.
	coach · stagecoach · cockroach · poached

2 Writing Words. On the lines below, write the words that you hear.

1. foam
2. toad
3. goal
4. loan
5. coal
6. road
7. boatload
8. toast
9. soak
10. coastline
11. overcoat
12. stagecoach

3 Using Sight Words. Fill in the blanks in the sentences below with the sight words from this lesson. Use each word only once. Your dictionary will help if you need to check the facts.

1. There are 12 inches in a ___foot___ and 36 inches in a ___yard___.

2. There are one hundred ___centimeters___ in a meter.

3. A ___meter___ is a little over 39 inches long.

4. There are one thousand meters in a ___kilometer___.

5. There are about two and one-half centimeters in an ___inch___.

Arrange the sight words in order from the smallest measure to the largest and write them on the lines below. The first one is done to get you started.

centimeter, inch, foot, yard, meter, kilometer

4 Finding a Pattern. In each pair of words, underline the word that has a long vowel sound.

1. cot — coat   2. road — rod   3. got — goat

What letter has been added to the underlined words to make the *o* long? ___a___

Where has the letter been added? ___after the o___

Can you hear the added letter in the underlined words? ___no___

What sound does *oa* make in the words above? ___long o sound.___

Pattern: The letters *oa* usually make the sound of long *o*.

Lesson 22   107

2 Writing Words

Instruct students to write the words that you dictate, which are found on the replica of the student page. Say each word, use it in a phrase or simple sentence, and say the word again.

3 Using Sight Words

Before students begin this exercise, help them locate the table of measurements in their dictionaries, if there is one. Some dictionaries have a table of measurements in an appendix; others have tables near the entries for *measurement, metric, length,* or *weight.*

Additional Activities:

Discuss the metric system briefly with students. Find out if they are studying it in another class. If they are, see if there are any materials that can be adapted for your use.

For more advanced students, discuss the meanings of the prefixes *kilo-* and *centi-.*

4 Finding a Pattern

In this exercise, students discover that the *oa* digraph produces the long *o*. After the exercise is completed, ask students what other pattern produces the long *o* (oCe). Ask them what they might expect to find when there are two common patterns which produce the same vowel sound. Students should be able to generalize about these patterns and expect some homonym pairs from the oaC and oCe families.

5 **Dictionary Skills: Abbreviations.** Write the abbreviation for each sight word on the lines provided. Use your dictionary if necessary.

1. centimeter ____cm____ 　　4. kilometer ____km____

2. foot ____ft____ 　　5. meter ____m____

3. inch ____in or in____ 　　6. yard ____yd____

6 **Dictionary Skills: Homonyms**

Part A. Answer the following questions, using a dictionary when you need to.

1. Is a car driven on a *road* or a *rode*? ____road____

2. Would you go to a bank for a *loan* or a *lone*? ____loan____

3. Is a vein of gold ore a *load* or a *lode*? ____lode____

4. Is *Roam* or *Rome* the capital of Italy? ____Rome____

Part B. Fill in each blank in the sentences below with the correct spelling of the phonetically spelled words.

1. /rōd/ Joe ____rode____ on the Long Island Rail____road____.

2. /lōd/ The miners took a ____load____ of silver from the mother ____lode____.

3. /rōm/ Cory ____roam____ed around Europe and ended up in ____Rome____.

4. /lōn/ Joan was the ____lone____ applicant to get a ____loan____.

7 **Hearing Differences.** Careless speaking and listening can result in poor spelling. Many words sound almost like other words. Listen carefully to the sets of words you hear. Then write the endings on the lines provided.

1. co__al____ 　co__ld____ 　　4. go__ad____ 　go__ld____

2. co__at____ 　co__lt____ 　　5. go__al____ 　go__ld____

3. co__de____ 　co__ld____ 　　6. to__ad____ 　to__ld____

5 **Dictionary Skills: Abbreviations**

You may want to do this exercise as a group activity.

Dictionaries differ on where they list abbreviations. Some dictionaries include them in the general alphabetical listing, while others have a special section for abbreviations either in the front or the back of the book. Help students to find where abbreviations are located in their dictionaries.

Discuss how abbreviations are generally formed before students begin the exercise. Note that most, but not all, abbreviations start with the initial letter of the word they stand for.

Tell students to look up the most likely spelling for each abbreviation first. They may have to try several possibilities before they find the correct one. For instance, the abbreviation for *centimeter* might be *c*, *C, c.*, *cm*, or *ct*. They should look up their best guess first.

There may be more than one correct abbreviation for some of these words. In addition, dictionaries may differ on whether or not the abbreviation needs a period. Accept all responses that students find in their dictionaries.

6 **Dictionary Skills: Homonyms**

In Part A of this exercise, students select the appropriate word from a pair of homonyms. In Part B, each homonym pair is used in a single sentence. Check to be sure students are using these words correctly.

7 **Hearing Differences**

Sometimes students misspell words because they are spelling words according to an incorrect pronunciation. This exercise contrasts oaC and oCe words with olC words.

8 **Creating Sentences.** Four different means of transportation are pictured below. Imagine that you have taken a trip using one of these methods of travel. On a separate sheet of paper, write a story describing your trip. Use some of the following long *o* words in your story.

stagecoach	road	coat	hope
boat	roam	load	before
railroad	rode	whole	postpone
carload	drove	alone	homesick

9 **Writing Sentences.** On the lines below, write the sentences that you hear.

1. A meter is about three inches longer than a yard.
2. We sailed the boat along the coast of Maine.
3. You'll have to soak that coat to get the stain out.
4. A whole carload of people just drove into Joan's driveway.
5. Remember to bring some charcoal so we can roast hot dogs.
6. They used railroad passes to roam around Spain last summer.
7. In the Old West, people took stagecoaches from place to place.
8. The coach groaned as Mike's try at a field goal missed by a foot.

Lesson 22   109

8 Creating Sentences

Discuss the illustrations with students to help them decide which method of transportation they want to write about. Some students may want to describe an actual trip they have taken. Others may prefer to write about an imaginary journey. Encourage them to use as many long *o* and sight words as they can.

9 Writing Sentences

Instruct students to write the sentences that you dictate, which are on the replica of the student page. Note any specific errors. Design additional sentences, words, or phrases for specific problems.

Patterns found in these sentences include:
—adding *-s* or *-es* (1, 5, 6, and 7)
—contractions (3)
—homonyms (2, 4, and 6)
—irregular verb forms (4 and 7)
—possession (4 and 8)

Lesson 23

The Word Families *o*, *oe*, *ow*, and *own*

Objectives

- **Word Families:** Learn to spell words in the *o, oe, ow,* and *own* families.
- **Sight Words:** Learn to spell *how, now, town, clown, howl,* and *towel.*
- **Dictionary Skills:** Learn to discriminate between pairs of homonyms.
  Learn to use the dictionary to determine the plural of words that end in *o.*
- **Patterns:** Learn to drop the silent *e* from words that end in *oe* when adding an ending that begins with a vowel other than *i* or *y.*
  Discover that a few words that end in *o* form the plural following predictable patterns.
- **Writing Sentences:** Practice writing word family and sight words in context.

Sight Words

Teach the sight words using the methods described on pages 9-12 in the introduction to this book. Point out the /ou/ pronunciation of the *ow* digraph in each of these words.

❶ Listening

Introduce the words in the *o* family using the following steps.

1. Say the sound /ō/ and ask students what letter makes the sound in the first group of words.
2. Say the letter *o* and ask students what sound it makes.
3. Say the word *omit* and ask students what letter spells /ō/ and what letters spell /mit/.
4. Say the word *omit* and ask students what letters spell *omit.*

Lesson 23

The Word Families *o*, *oe*, *ow*, and *own*

Sight Words

how	town	howl
now	clown	towel

Word Families

o

❶ Listening

Listen to the sound *o* makes in these words.

omit	go	so	local
over	ago	sofa	locate
obey	piano	solo	donate
ocean	radio	Soviet	program

oe

Listen to the sound *oe* makes in these words.

doe	foe	toe
hoe	woe	tiptoe
Joe	goes	oboe

ow

Listen to the sound *ow* makes in these words.

low	row	tow	narrow
blow	crow	know	shadow
below	grow	show	window
slowly	throw	snowflake	rainbow
overflow	borrow	elbow	tomorrow

own

Listen to the sound *own* makes in these words.

own	blown	known	grown
ownership	flown	shown	thrown

110   Lesson 23

Note the long *a* pronunciation of the digraph *ey* in *obey.*

Follow the same steps to introduce the words in the *oe, ow,* and *own* families.

When you have introduced the words in the *ow* family, contrast their pronunciation with the sight words *how, now, howl,* and *towel.* You might want to point out that there are a few words, such as *bow* and *row,* that can be pronounced both ways.

Contrast the sight words *town* and *clown* with words in the *own* family.

Point out the silent *k* in *know* and *known.* Discuss the relationship between *know* and *known.* Ask students to find four other pairs of family words that have the same relationship (*blow/blown, grow/ grown, throw/thrown,* and *show/ shown*). If students are keeping a table of irregular verbs, have them add these to the list. Have them look up the past tense forms if necessary.

2 Writing Words. On the lines below, write the words that you hear.

1. toe
2. local
3. below
4. known
5. radio
6. open
7. slowly
8. grown
9. donate
10. throw
11. ownership
12. borrow

3 Dictionary Skills: Homonyms. Answer the following questions using a dictionary if necessary.

1. Is a female deer a *doe* or a *dough*?   doe
2. If something has gotten bigger, has it *groan* or *grown*?   grown
3. Does a king sit on a *throne* or a *thrown*?   throne
4. When you plant seeds, do you *so* them or *sow* them?   sow
5. Do you *no* or *know* how to do something?   know
6. Has the movie been *shone* or *shown* many times?   shown

4 Adding Endings to Words That End in *o* or *oe*. Generally, when endings are added to words that end in *o*, no letters are added, dropped, or changed.

    Examples: radio + ed = radioed   solo + ist = soloist

When endings are added to words that end in *oe*, the silent *e* is dropped if the ending begins with any vowel except *i* or *y*.

    Examples: hoe + ed = hoed   tiptoe + ing = tiptoeing

Add the endings to the words below.

1. echo + ing   echoing
2. hero + ic   heroic
3. Joe + y   Joey
4. canoe + ed   canoed
5. veto + ing   vetoing
6. woe + ful + ly   woefully
7. canoe + ing   canoeing
8. toe + hold   toehold

Lesson 23   111

2 Writing Words

Instruct students to write the words that you dictate, which are found on the replica of the student page. Say each word, use it in a phrase or simple sentence, and say the word again.

3 Dictionary Skills: Homonyms

When students have finished this exercise, discuss the meaning of the other homonym in each pair. Be sure students know the meaning of both homonyms in each pair.

If students have trouble distinguishing between *shone* and *shown* in number 6, point out that both of these words are past participles of irregular verbs. Tell them to think of the present tense form of each verb. They should ask themselves if we *shine* a movie or *show* a movie.

4 Adding Endings to Words That End in *o* or *oe*

People often have trouble spelling words that end in *o* or *oe*, particularly when suffixes are added. This is partly because even when the words are spelled correctly they tend to "look funny." Stress the fact that in most cases endings are added to these words in the regular way, i.e., nothing is changed or dropped when the root word ends in *o*, but the silent *e* is dropped from words that end in *oe* if an ending begins with a vowel. The only exception to the rules that they have been practicing throughout this book is that if an ending begins with *i* or *y*, the *e* is retained in words that end in *oe*.

5 **Plurals of Words Ending with *o*.** Some words that end in *o* have -*s* added to form the plural. Others have -*es* added. For some words, either -*s* or -*es* can be added. Look up the following words in the dictionary and write their plural forms in the appropriate columns.

	Add -*s*	Add -*es*
1. video	videos	
2. ratio	ratios	
3. patio	patios	
4. stereo	stereos	
5. radio	radios	
6. trio	trios	
7. echo		echoes
8. veto		vetoes
9. hero		heroes
10. tomato		tomatoes
11. potato		potatoes
12. piano	pianos	
13. solo	solos	
14. alto	altos	
15. soprano	sopranos	
16. zero	zeros	zeroes
17. tornado	tornados	tornadoes
18. volcano	volcanos	volcanoes

5 **Plurals of Words Ending with *o***

In this exercise, students are asked to look up words that end in *o* to find whether the plurals are formed by adding -*s* or -*es*. You may want them to work in pairs or small groups, since there are so many words to look up. Point out that when no plural is given after the entry word, the plural is formed by adding -*s*.

Some students may be confused by an apparent contradiction between Exercises 4 and 5. Exercise 4 states that, in general, no letters are added, dropped, or changed when endings are added to words that end in *o*. Point out that when forming the plural of these words, we are not adding an *e* to some of these words. Instead we are choosing between two possible endings, -*s* or -*es*.

6 Finding Patterns. Fill in the blanks below to discover two patterns which will help you to know whether to add -*s* or -*es* to form the plural of words ending in *o*.

Part A. Write the plurals of the words from Exercise 5 that end with two vowels.

1. videos   3. patios   5. radios
2. ratios   4. stereos   6. trios

Pattern: Add ___s___ to form the plural of words that end with Vo.

Part B. Write the plurals of words in the field of music (*piano, solo, alto* and *soprano*).

pianos   solos   altos   sopranos

Pattern: Add ___s___ to form the plural of words ending with *o* from the field of music.

Part C. Following the patterns above, write the plural of these words:

1. curio   curios   4. banjo   banjos
2. rodeo   rodeos   5. piccolo   piccolos
3. studio   studios   6. cello   cellos

7 Writing Sentences. On the lines below, write the sentences that you hear.

1. Will you please open the windows?
2. How will you know when we are ready to come home?
3. Now I know where to take my sofa to have it repaired.
4. Everyone enrolled in that program finishes it tomorrow.
5. The clown wiped the makeup from his face with a towel.
6. That store sold everything from radios and stereos to videos.
7. I've known about Joe's broken toes since he told me two days ago.
8. The tornado howled through the town blowing down everything in its path.

6 Finding Patterns

It is difficult to generalize about how to form the plurals of words that end in *o*, because the choice often seems completely arbitrary. However, as students discover in this exercise, a few groups of words do follow regular patterns. Words that end in **V**o tend to have -*s* added. Most music-related words that end in *o* also have -*s* added.

Tell students that in order to be sure of whether to add -*s* or -*es* to words that end in *o*, they will probably have to use a dictionary.

7 Writing Sentences

Instruct students to write the sentences that you dictate, which are on the replica of the student page. Note any specific errors. Design additional sentences, words, or phrases for specific problems.

Patterns found in these sentences include:

—adding -*s* or -*es* (1, 4, 6, and 7)
—homonyms (2, 3, and 7)
—alternative spellings for /ōld/ (4, 6, and 7)
—Silent *e* Pattern 1 (5)
—irregular verb forms (6 and 7)
—possession (7)
—contractions (7)

Review of Unit 4
The Long *o*

1 **Word Building with oCe Families.** Add one of the word families listed below to each of the consonants to make a word. Do not make the same word twice.

ope	ome	ote	ose
one	ove	ode	oze
oke	obe	ore	ole

1. c_ope_____   8. p_ole_____   15. cl_ose_____
2. h_ome_____   9. r_ode_____   16. fr_oze_____
3. j_oke_____   10. r_obe_____   17. gr_ope_____
4. l_one_____   11. t_one_____   18. sp_oke_____
5. m_ore_____   12. v_ote_____   19. st_ove_____
6. n_ote_____   13. w_oke_____   20. st_one_____
7. n_ose_____   14. z_one_____   21. wh_ole_____

2 **Other Patterns for Spelling Long *o*.** One pattern that produces long *o* is oCe. Six other patterns which you learned in Unit 4 are listed below. Write three words for each pattern.

1. olC _____ _____ _____
2. oaC _____ _____ _____
3. o _____ _____ _____
4. oe _____ _____ _____
5. ow _____ _____ _____
6. own _____ _____ _____

Review of Unit 4
The Long *o*

Objectives

- **Word Building:** Add oCe families to initial consonants, blends, and digraphs.
- **Patterns:** Review six other patterns which produce long *o*.
- **Dictionary Skills:** Find the principal parts of irregular verbs.
- **Irregular Verbs:** Use irregular verb forms to complete sentences.
- **Alternative Spellings:** Review the alternative spellings of /ōl/, /ōld/, and /ōz/.
- **Writing by Syllables:** Write dictated words by syllables.
- **Writing Sentences:** Practice writing word family and sight words in context.
- **Puzzle:** Review long *o* family words and sight words by completing a crossword puzzle.

1 **Word Building with oCe Families**

Have students add one of the word families to each consonant, blend, or digraph to make a word. Encourage them to use all of the word families at least once. The answers given on the replica of the student page are examples. Accept all correctly spelled words. If students form *love* for number 4 or *move* for number 5, accept them as correctly spelled words, and point out the difference in pronunciation from the *ove* family words.

2 **Other Patterns for Spelling Long *o***

This exercise reviews the other patterns for spelling long *o* that students learned in this unit. Pay particular attention to the words students write for the *ow* and *own* families. Be sure these words are pronounced /ō/ rather than /ou/.

130   Review of Unit 4

3 **Dictionary Skills: Irregular Verbs.** Write the forms of the verbs below in the appropriate columns. Use your dictionary if necessary.

Present Tense	Past Tense	*Have*, *Has*, or *Had* + Verb	*-ing* Form of Verb
1. go	went	gone	going
2. fly	flew	flown	flying
3. blow	blew	blown	blowing
4. grow	grew	grown	growing
5. know	knew	known	knowing

4 **Using Irregular Verbs.** Fill in the sentences below with the correct form of the verb in parentheses.

1. (sell)   Rose _____ sold _____ her old sofa at the garage sale.

2. (tell)   Doreen _____ told _____ me she couldn't baby-sit today.

3. (hold)   Joe _____ held _____ on to the tow rope after he fell into the water.

4. (break)   Tony _____ broke _____ Owen's record in the high jump yesterday.

5. (speak)   Have you _____ spoken _____ to Norman about going to the movies with us?

6. (choose)   I wanted cheesecake for dessert, but Cory _____ chose _____ apple pie.

7. (freeze)   Grove's Pond was _____ frozen _____ for four months last winter.

8. (wear)   The neighborhood kids have _____ worn _____ a path across our yard.

9. (tear)   Joan _____ tore _____ up the letter and threw it away.

10. (throw)   All of the magazines that you saved got _____ thrown _____ out by mistake.

5 **Writing Words.** On the lines below, write the words that you hear.

1. stole	4. enrolled	7. toll
2. scold	5. expose	8. swollen
3. froze	6. bold	9. suppose

Review of Unit 4   115

---

3 **Dictionary Skills: Irregular Verbs**

All of the verbs in this exercise have at least one principal part that contains a long *o* family. Allow students to use their dictionaries to look up the principal parts if they need to. Point out that, with the exception of *go*, all of these verbs form their principal parts following the same pattern, i.e., the past tense is spelled with *ew* and the past participle is spelled with *own*. Note that *throw*, which is not included in this exercise, follows the same patterns.

If students are keeping a table of irregular verbs in their notebooks, have them add these to the list.

4 **Using Irregular Verbs**

In this exercise, students complete sentences with some of the irregular verbs covered in Unit 4. They must select the principal part of the verb that is appropriate in the context of the sentence. *Tear* is being introduced for the first time. Allow students to look it up in their dictionaries if they need to. Also, have them add it to their list of irregular verbs.

5 **Writing Words**

Instruct students to write the words that you dictate, which are found on the replica of the student page. Say each word, use it in a phrase or simple sentence, and say the word again. The purpose of this exercise is to see if students are able to spell correctly words containing $/\bar{o}l/$, $/\bar{o}ld/$, and $/\bar{o}z/$.

6 **Writing Words by Syllables.** Write the words your teacher dictates by syllables. Then write the entire word on the line provided.

	First Syllable	Second Syllable	Third Syllable	Fourth Syllable	Whole Word
1.	re	proach			reproach
2.	dis	pos	al		disposal
3.	post	pone	ment		postponement
4.	ob	so	lete		obsolete
5.	ad	vo	cate		advocate
6.	ex	plor	er		explorer
7.	mi	cro	scope		microscope
8.	his	to	ri	an	historian

7 **Writing Sentences.** On the lines below, write the sentences that you hear.

1. The whole lake froze over in January.
2. Joan wore a coat made of yellow cloth.
3. Mrs. Price has grown oats for many years now.
4. After Flo added the yeast, the dough rose.
5. Joe was hoping his microscope hadn't been broken.
6. When Bill stepped on the hoe, it struck him on the elbow.
7. Kate chose the wrong road when she drove to the coast.
8. As we strolled along the shoreline, the sun went down.
9. All the coaches boasted about how well their own teams played.
10. When the flames died down, we roasted potatoes on the smoldering coals.

6 **Writing Words by Syllables**

Dictate each word by syllables, emphasizing the syllables. Then pronounce the whole word normally. Remind students that the number of blanks indicates the number of syllables in the word.

If students have difficulty spelling words with many syllables, have them identify the syllable types. Encourage them to pronounce the words syllable by syllable.

Additional Activities:

Have students look up the meanings of any of these words that they don't already know.

Have them use some of the words in original sentences.

7 **Writing Sentences**

Instruct students to write the sentences that you dictate, which are on the replica of the student page. Note any specific errors. Design additional sentences, words, or phrases for specific problems.

Patterns found in these sentences include:
—irregular verb forms (1, 2, 3, 4, 5, 6, 7, and 8)
—homonyms (1, 3, 4, 7, and 9)
—double consonants in the middle of words (2)
—adding -s or -es (3, 9, and 10)
—Silent e Pattern 1 (5)
—contractions (5)
—Doubling Pattern 1 (6)

8 **Crossword Puzzle.** Use the clues below to complete the puzzle. Most of the answers are word family or sight words from Unit 4.

Across

1. A tool used by farmers and gardeners
2. You can call long distance on these.
6. Filled with fluid: His sprained ankle is ____.
7. A letter is mailed in this.
10. What we breathe
12. A homonym for or
13. A flowing garment used as a coat
15. Past tense of do
16. To nap; to sleep lightly
17. The opposite of yes
18. People cook on these.
21. A passage inside the neck
24. Past tense of weave
25. Healthy, nourishing

Down

1. A male spouse
2. This is used to see stars.
3. The only one
4. To irritate or make angry
5. To run off and get married
8. Something carried; a burden
9. Indicates a choice: either this ____ that
11. An instrument used to receive broadcasts
14. Possess: Do you ____ your home?
18. To explain or display: ____ and tell
19. To go to the polls to elect someone
20. What rain becomes in winter
21. A charge for using a bridge or highway
22. Uses oars to move the boat
23. A sound having a certain quality: a pleasant ____ of voice

8 **Crossword Puzzle**

Encourage students to use the length of the words as additional clues for solving the puzzle. If necessary, provide them with the following list of answer words. Tell them to cross off words as they use them.

air	radio
cloak	rows
did	show
doze	snow
elope	stoves
envelope	swollen
hoe	telephones
husband	telescope
load	throat
lone	toll
no	tone
or	vote
ore	wholesome
own	wove
provoke	

Unit 4 Tests

We recommend that you test your students on the word family and sight words from Unit 4 before going on. The following are suggested lists of representative family words and sight words from Unit 4. You may wish to substitute other words to meet the needs of your students. Dictate each word and use it in a simple sentence. Students should be able to spell 90 percent of these words correctly.

Family Words	**Sight Words**
1. cold	1. inch
2. nose	2. how
3. roll	3. women
4. alone	4. most
5. goal	5. hurry
6. store	6. all right
7. coach	7. town
8. loan	8. foot
9. broke	9. always
10. omit	10. cloth
11. boast	11. spouse
12. goes	12. already
13. drove	13. spirit
14. frozen	14. worry
15. voter	15. meter
16. show	16. husband
17. overcoat	17. yard
18. owner	18. promise
19. wholesome	19. towel
20. shadow	20. during

Review of Book 2

The Long Vowel Word Families

Syllable Type	Long a Lessons 1-6	Long e Lessons 7-14		Long i Lessons 15-18	Long o Lessons 19-23
VCe				ibe	obe
	ace			ice	
	ade			ide	ode
	afe			ife	
	age				
	ake			ike	oke
	ale			ile	ole
	ame			ime	ome
	ane			ine	one
	ape			ipe	ope
	are			ire	ore
	ase			ise	ose
	ate			ite	ote
	ave			ive	ove
	aze			ize	oze
VVC		eech	each		oach
or	aid	eed	ead		oad
VVCC		eek	eak		oak
	ail	eel	eal		oal
	aim	eem	eam		oam
	ain	een	ean		oan
	aint				
		eep	eap		
	air	eer	ear		
			east		oast
	ait	eet	eat		oat
V or VV	ay	e		y	o
		ea			oe
		ee			
		ey			
		y			
Other Syllables	aise	ease		igh	old
	ange	eeze		ight	oll
	aste	eave		ign	olt
	ary	ceive		ild	ow
	azy	ly		ind	own

Review of Book 2

Objectives

- **Long Vowel Families:** Review common patterns that produce long vowel sounds.
  Review alternative spellings for some long vowel combinations.
- **Endings:** Review six patterns for adding endings.
  Add endings to words following these patterns.
- **Syllable Types:** Review five types of syllables.
- **Writing by Syllables:** Write dictated words by syllables.
- **Word Building:** Build words by combining syllables.
- **Irregular Verbs:** Use irregular verb forms to complete sentences.
- **Creating Sentences:** Use homonym pairs in original sentences.
- **Puzzle:** Review word family and sight words by completing a crossword puzzle.

The Long Vowel Word Families

This chart presents the families covered in this text in a form that lets students see relationships among the word families. Some families share the same consonant endings and differ only in their initial vowel or vowel combination. Draw students' attention to the *ade*, *ide*, and *ode* families and to the *aid*, *eed*, *ead*, and *oad* families as examples.

Note also items that are missing from the chart. Point out particularly that there are no eCe families nor any double vowel families that produce long *i*. Explain to students that, while there are some words that follow those patterns, the patterns are much less common than the ones included in the chart.

❶ Patterns for Spelling Long Vowels. Several ways to spell each of the long vowels are represented on the chart. Write one word that uses each of the spellings given below.

Long a

1. aCe _____ 3. ay _____ 5. ange _____
2. aiC _____ 4. aCy _____ 6. aste _____

Long e

1. e _____ 4. eaC _____ 7. eCe _____
2. ee _____ 5. ea _____ 8. y _____
3. eeC _____ 6. ey _____ 9. ly _____

Long i

1. iCe _____ 3. ign _____ 5. iCd _____
2. igh _____ 4. y _____ 6. ight _____

Long o

1. oCe _____ 3. olC _____ 5. oe _____
2. oaC _____ 4. o _____ 6. ow _____

❷ Writing Words. On the lines below, write the words that you hear.

1. doze
2. expose
3. race
4. eraser
5. speak
6. speech
7. tiptoe
8. became
9. price
10. prize
11. surprise
12. increase
13. scold
14. rolled
15. paroled
16. reclaim
17. please
18. receive

Review of Book 2   119

❶ Patterns for Spelling Long Vowels

Before students begin this exercise, remind them that **C** stands for any consonant. You may want to allow them to use the word lists at the back of the book if they need to. The eCe words will not be included there, however.

Check to be sure that for number 8 under Long *e*, the word selected uses *y* to spell long *e* rather than long *i* (e.g., *many*). On the other hand, for number 4 under Long *i*, the word selected should use *y* to spell long *i* (e.g., *fly*).

❷ Writing Words

Instruct students to write the words that you dictate, which are found on the replica of the student page. Say each word, use it in a phrase or simple sentence, and say the word again. This exercise contrasts some of the alternative spelling patterns covered in this text, such as *oze/ose*, *ace/ase*, *ea/ee*, aCe/aiC, *ice/ise/ize*, and *old/olled/oled*.

❸ Reviewing Patterns for Endings. Fill in the blanks below to review the patterns you have learned for adding endings.

1. **Doubling Pattern 1.** Double the final consonant if a word has one __syllable__, one __vowel__, and one __final__ consonant, and the ending begins with a __vowel__. Do not double __w__ or *x*.

2. **Silent *e* Pattern 1.** Drop a silent *e* at the end of a word if the ending begins with a __vowel__.

3. **The Ending *-es*.** When a word ends in *s*, __x__, *z*, __ch__, or __sh__, add *-es* instead of *-s* to form the plural.

4. **Changing *y* to *i*.** When a word ends in C*y*, change the *y* to *i* before adding any ending that doesn't begin with __i__. Add __es__ instead of *-s* to form the plural.

5. **Changing *f* to *v*.** To form the plural of some words that end in *f* or *fe*, change the *f* or *fe* to __v__ and add __es__.

6. **Words That End in *o* and *oe*.** Words that end in __o__ are not changed when endings are added. Some words that end in *o* have *-s* added to form the plural, while others have __es__ added. Words that end in *oe* drop the silent *e* if an ending begins with any __vowel__ except *i* or *y*.

❹ Adding Endings. Add the endings to the words below.

1. hurry + ing	hurrying	8. beach + s *or* es	beaches
2. quote + able	quotable	9. journey + s *or* es	journeys
3. tow + ed	towed	10. worry + ed	worried
4. delay + ed	delayed	11. desire + able	desirable
5. radio + s *or* es	radios	12. hoe + ing	hoeing
6. hop + ing	hopping	13. knife + s *or* es	knives
7. hope + ing	hoping	14. like + ly + est	likeliest

❸ Reviewing Patterns for Endings

This exercise reviews six patterns for adding endings that students have learned in Books 1 and 2. Be sure students remember these patterns and understand how to use them.

❹ Adding Endings

In this exercise, students demonstrate their ability to use the six patterns reviewed in Exercise 3. Note any patterns that are still troublesome and provide extra practice as needed.

5 **Review of Syllable Types.** Write one example of each of the five syllable types presented in this book.

1. Closed _____   3. Cle _____   5. Double Vowel _____

2. Open _____   4. VCe _____

6 **Writing Words by Syllables.** Write the words that you hear one syllable at a time. Then write the whole word on the line at the right. Use the syllable types to help you spell the word.

	First Syllable	Second Syllable	Third Syllable	Fourth Syllable	Whole Word
1.	ob	so	lete		obsolete
2.	main	te	nance		maintenance
3.	re	place	ment		replacement
4.	nom	i	nate		nominate
5.	o	ver	weight		overweight
6.	re	cy	cle		recycle
7.	im	me	di	ate	immediate
8.	re	li	a	able	reliable

7 **Word Building.** Add a syllable from Column 2 to a syllable in Column 1 to make a word. Write the words on the lines provided. Use each syllable only once.

Column 1	Column 2	Words
sea	ley	1. season
val	dy	2. valley
mud	son	3. muddy
pre	ro	4. prefix
he	fix	5. hero

---

5 **Review of Syllable Types**

If necessary, review the attributes of the five types of syllables covered in this text before students do this exercise. The answers on the replica of the student page are examples. Accept all correct responses.

6 **Writing Words by Syllables**

Dictate each word by syllables, emphasizing the syllables. Then pronounce the whole word normally. Remind students that the number of blanks indicates the number of syllables in the word.

7 **Word Building**

In this exercise, students are asked to combine syllables to form words. Tell students to check off the syllables as they use them.

8 **Using Irregular Verbs.** Fill in the blank in each sentence below with the correct form of the verb in parentheses.

1. (go)   Gail has ____gone____ to the store to get some milk.

2. (hear)   Have you ____heard____ the news about Joe's promotion?

3. (hide)   Amy can't remember where she ____hid____ her diary.

4. (give)   Gary ____gave____ Joan a ring for her birthday.

5. (mean)   Did you figure out what Lee ____meant____ when he said that?

6. (strike) The car ____struck____ the telephone pole, but no one was hurt.

7. (come)   Jean ____came____ to the apartment shortly after you left.

8. (know)   Steve has ____known____ Ray since they were in elementary school.

9. (speak)   Tony has ____spoken____ to the neighbors about the noise several times.

10. (eat)   I hope they haven't ____eaten____ all the cake by the time we get there.

9 **Reviewing Homonyms.** Write a sentence using each of the following homonyms.

1. hole   _____
2. whole   _____
3. meat   _____
4. meet   _____
5. plane   _____
6. plain   _____
7. steal   _____
8. steel   _____
9. waist   _____
10. waste   _____

8 Using Irregular Verbs

In this exercise, students use some of the most common irregular verbs covered in this text. They must select the principal part that is appropriate in the context of the sentence. Provide additional practice for students who have trouble with this exercise.

9 Reviewing Homonyms

In this exercise, students use five sets of common homonyms in original sentences. Check to be sure they are using the homonyms correctly in their sentences. Errors in words that haven't been studied shouldn't be treated negatively. Point out any parts of the word that are spelled correctly and praise the effort.

⑩ Crossword Puzzle. Use the clues below to complete the puzzle. The answers are all word family or sight words from this text.

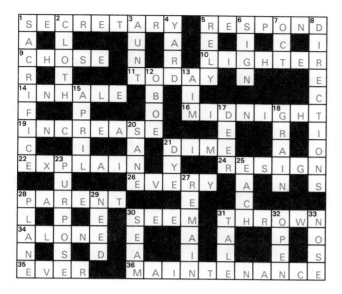

Across

1. The officer of a club who takes notes and keeps minutes
5. To answer
9. Selected
10. Not as dark
11. The day before tomorrow
14. To breathe in
16. The middle of the night
19. Opposite of decrease
21. Two nickles equals one ___.
22. To give reasons for
24. To give up one's job or position
26. Each
28. Mother or father
30. To appear to be
31. Homonym of throne
34. All by yourself
35. Always: forever and ___
36. The work of keeping something in good repair

Down

1. Give up: I decided to ___ my free weekend to help John move.
2. Material for making clothes
3. Your father's sister
4. Three feet
5. Depend on
6. A signal: a stop ___
7. Abbreviation for October
8. Instructions on how to do something
12. A woodwind instrument
13. A purpose or goal: His ___ is to pass this course.
15. The fourth month
17. An animal that lives in forests
18. The seed of a cereal plant such as wheat
20. Mentally healthy; sensible
21. To change the color of something
23. The reason for something: What is the ___ of this meeting?
25. Every
27. To stay in a place
28. This flies through the sky.
29. Require: I ___ eight hours of sleep.
30. A homonym for seem
31. A story: A fairy ___
32. The opposite of closed
33. This is in the middle of a face.

Review of Book 2 123

⑩ Crossword Puzzle

Encourage students to use word length as an additional clue. If necessary, supply students with the following list of answer words. Tell them to cross off words as they use them.

aim	each	need
alone	ever	nose
April	every	oboe
aunt	explain	Oct.
chose	grain	open
cloth	increase	parent
deer	inhale	plane
dime	lighter	purpose
directions	maintenance	rely
dye	midnight	remain

resign	secretary	tale
respond	seam	thrown
sacrifice	seem	today
sane	sign	yard

Book 2 Tests

We recommend that you test your students on the word family and sight words from Book 2 before going on to Book 3. The following are suggested lists of representative family words and sight words. If students have had trouble with any of the word families, patterns, sounds, or sight words in this review of Book 2, you may wish to substitute other words to meet the needs of your students.

Dictate each word and use it in a simple sentence. Students should be able to spell 90 percent of these words correctly.

Sight Words

1. length	14. south
2. enough	15. answer
3. floor	16. now
4. beauty	17. color
5. almost	18. though
6. February	19. kilometer
7. fluid	20. people
8. heart	21. thorough
9. parent	22. trouble
10. woman	23. question
11. very	24. all right
12. soul	25. country
13. machine	

Family Words

1. treat	26. weekend
2. mind	27. locate
3. pair	28. reason
4. greet	29. sailboat
5. trace	30. mistake
6. plead	31. notebook
7. needle	32. beyond
8. lonely	33. tonight
9. escape	34. railroad
10. truly	35. stovepipe
11. teacher	36. agreed
12. daily	37. suppose
13. thrown	38. meanwhile
14. contain	39. fifteen
15. valley	40. sunshine
16. female	41. deceive
17. coaster	42. overtime
18. cease	43. keyhole
19. share	44. bravery
20. swollen	45. engagement
21. snowflake	46. shoreline
22. graceful	47. doorkeeper
23. retired	48. alphabetize
24. appear	49. necessary
25. despise	50. blindfold

Word Families and Representative Words

Lesson 1

ake
awake
bake
baker
brake
brake fluid
cake
mistake
shake
snake
stake
take
wake

ame
became
blame
came
flame
frame
framed
name
same

ade
grade
lemonade
made
parade
shade
spade
trade
wade

ate
ate
exaggerate
fascinate
fate
gate
late
lately
later
locate
plate
state
United States

age
age
cage
engage

engagement
page
stage
teenager
wage

Lesson 2

ane
airplane
cane
insane
Jane
lane
mane
plane
sane
vane

ale
ale
female
inhale
male
pale
sale
salesperson
scale
tale

ave
behave
brave
cave
forgave
gave
grave
pave
save

afe
chafe
safe
safely
safety

aste
haste
paste
taste
waste

Lesson 3

ase
base

basement
case
chase
eraser
vase

ace
bracelet
disgrace
face
graceful
lace
misplace
pace
place
race
space
trace

aze
amaze
amazement
blaze
craze
daze
gaze
haze
maze

ange
arrange
change
danger
dangerous
exchange
range
strange
stranger

ape
cape
drape
escape
grape
scrape
scraper
shape
tape

Lesson 4

ail
ail
daily
detail

fail
Gail
mail
nail
pail
rail
railroad
retail
sail
sailor
tail
tailor
trail

aim
aim
aimless
claim
maim
reclaim

ain
complain
contain
entertainment
explain
gain
maintain
maintenance
obtain
pain
plain
rain
remain
retain
stain
strain
train

ait
bait
trait
wait
waiter

Lesson 5

aid
afraid
aid
braid
braided
laid
maid
paid

prepaid
raid

air
air
chair
fair
flair
hair
pair
repair
stairs

aise
appraisal
appraise
mayonnaise
praise
raise

aint
acquaint
acquaintance
complaint
faint
paint
restraint

Lesson 6

ay
anyway
away
day
delay
display
highway
okay
pay
payday
payment
play
portray
repay
say
stay
way

are
bare
care
fare
flare
rare
share

silverware
welfare

ary
imaginary
library
literary
necessary
primary
scary
secondary
solitary
temporary
vary
vocabulary
voluntary

azy
crazy
hazy
lazy

Lesson 7

e
be
being
beyond
ego
equal
he
legal
maybe
me
prefix
react
senior

ee
agree
bee
coffee
fee
flee
free
freedom
knee
needle
see
three
tree

eer
beer
cheer

deer
pioneer
steer
volunteer

Lesson 8

eek
cheek
creek
Greek
peek
seek
sleek
week
weekend

eel
feel
heel
kneel
peel
steel
wheel

eet
beet
feet
fleet
greet
meeting
sheet
sleet
sweet

eem
esteem
redeem
seem

Lesson 9

een
between
canteen
fifteen
fourteen
green
keen
queen
screen
seen
teen
teenager
thirteen

eed
agreed
bleed
deed
feed
greed
indeed
need
proceed
seed
speed
succeed
weed

eep
asleep
creep
deep
doorkeeper
jeep
keep
peep
sheep
sleep
steep
sweep
weep

eech
screech
speech
speechless

Lesson 10

ea
eager
measles
pea
plea
reason
sea
season
tea
teaspoon

ead
bead
lead
plead
read

eak
creak
leak
peak
sneakers
speak

squeak
streak
weak

eam
beam
cream
dream
scream
seam
steam
stream
team

Lesson 11

eat
beat
cheat
defeat
eat
heat
heater
meat
neat
repeat
seat
treat
wheat

eal
appeal
conceal
deal
heal
meal
real
reveal
seal
steal

ean
bean
clean
dean
Jean
lean
mean

eap
cheap
heap
leap

Lesson 12

each
beach

bleach
each
impeach
impeachment
peach
preach
reach
teach
teacher
unbleached

east
beast
east
feast
least

ear
appear
clear
dear
disappear
ear
fear
hear
near
rear
shears
weary
year

Lesson 13

eeze
breeze
freeze
sneeze
squeeze

ease
cease
crease
decrease
disease
displease
ease
grease
increase
please
release
tease

eave
heave
leave
leaves
weave

ceive
conceive
deceive
receive

Lesson 14

ey
hockey
honey
jersey
journey
key
kidney
money
monkey
valley
volleyball

y
any
bravery
greasy
greedy
icy
recovery
secretary
shady
sleepy
study
wavy

ly
daily
doubly
gently
jelly
lately
lonely
Molly
really
truly
ugly

Lesson 15

ime
chime
crime
dime
grime
overtime
prime
slime
sometimes
time

ibe
bribe
describe
prescribe
tribe

ike
alike
bike
dike
hike
like
Mike
spike
strike

ice
advice
device
ice
mice
nice
price
rice
sacrifice
slice
twice

ipe
gripe
pipeline
ripe
stripe
swipe
wipe

ile
awhile
file
meanwhile
mile
pile
smile
tile
while

Lesson 16

ine
combine
decline
define
dine
fine
line
mine
shine
spine

sunshine
Valentine
whine

ire
admire
bonfire
desire
entire
expire
fire
hire
inquire
require
retired
tire
wire

ide
beside
bride
decide
divide
hide
pride
provide
ride
side
slide
tide
wide

ite
bite
excite
excitement
ignite
invite
kite
quite
recite
unexcited
unite
white
write

ife
knife
life
lifetime
wife

ive
alive
drive
driveway
hive

live
thrive

Lesson 17

ise
advertise
advise
arise
despise
disguise
exercise
revise
rise
supervise
surprise
wise

ize
alphabetize
criticize
memorize
prize
realize
recognize
size

y
apply
cry
deny
dry
fry
identify
rely
reply
shy
supply
try
why

Lesson 18

ight
bright
delight
fight
flashlight
light
midnight
might
night
right
sight
tight
tonight

igh

highway
sigh
thigh

ign
align
assign
benign
design
resign
sign

ind
behind
bind
blind
find
kind
kindness
mind
remind

ild
child
grandchild
mild
wild

Lesson 19

ope
cope
envelope
hope
rope
slope
telescope

one
alone
bone
lone
lonely
phone
postpone
shone
stone
telephone
tone
zone

oke
broke
broken
joke
poke
provoke
revoke

smoke
spoke
stroke
woke

ome
dome
home
homeless
homesick
Nome
Rome

ove
cove
drove
grove
rove
stove
stovepipe
strove
wove

Lesson 20

obe
globe
lobe
probe
robe
strobe

ote
devote
note
notebook
quote
remote
vote
voter
wrote

ode
code
erode
explode
mode
rode
zip code

ore
before
chore
core
folklore
moreover
ore
restore

shore
shoreline
sore
store
tore

ose
chose
close
disclose
expose
hose
nose
pose
rose
suppose
those

oze
bulldozer
doze
froze
frozen

Lesson 21

ole
buttonhole
hole
keyhole
mole
parole
pole
role
sole
stole
whole
wholesale
wholesome

oll
enroll
knoll
poll
roll
stroll
swollen
toll
wholly

old
blindfold
bold
cold
golden
hold
scold
sold

told
withhold

olt
bolt
colt
jolted
revolt
voltage

Lesson 22

oat
boat
coat
float
gloat
oats
overcoat
sailboat
throat

oam
foam
roam
styrofoam

oal
charcoal
coal
field goal
goal

oad
carload
goad
load
railroad
road
toad

oan
groan
Joan
loan
moan

oak
cloak
croak
oak
soak

oast
boast
coast
coastal

coaster
coastline
roller coaster
roast
toast

oach
coach
cockroach
poached
stagecoach

Lesson 23

o
ago
donate
go
local
locate
obey
ocean
omit
over
piano
program
radio
so
sofa
solo
Soviet

oe
doe
foe
goes
hoe
Joe
oboe
tiptoe
toe
woe

ow
below
blow
borrow
crow
elbow
grow
know
low
narrow
overflow
rainbow
row
shadow
show

slowly
snowflake
throw
tomorrow
tow
window

own
blown
flown
grown
known
own
ownership
shown
thrown

Sight Words

Sight Word	Lesson Number	Sight Word	Lesson Number	Sight Word	Lesson Number	Sight Word	Lesson Number
add	5	especially	7	ounce	17	west	3
all right	19	every	5	owe	10	western	3
almost	19	faith	5	oz.	17	wolf	11
already	19	father	14	parent	14	woman	20
although	9	February	1	people	4	women	20
altogether	18	ferry	6	person	4	worry	20
always	19	find	4	pound	17	yard	22
answer	15	flood	8	pretty	5	young	13
April	1	floor	18	promise	21		
August	2	fluid	17	prove	7		
aunt	14	foot	22	purpose	11		
beauty	5	group	16	question	15		
beef	8	half	8	ready	19		
been	12	heart	8	rhyme	15		
berry	6	hero	13	rough	9		
blood	8	how	23	route	16		
board	15	howl	23	September	2		
bored	15	hurry	20	shoulder	16		
both	15	husband	20	skiing	21		
broad	12	inch	22	sleeve	13		
bury	11	January	1	soul	21		
busy	11	July	2	south	3		
calf	8	June	1	southern	3		
canoe	21	kilometer	22	special	7		
carry	6	lb.	17	spirit	21		
centimeter	22	leaf	12	spouse	20		
cheese	13	leash	12	straight	18		
cloth	21	length	7	strength	7		
clothes	12	liquid	17	style	18		
clown	23	loose	4	sugar	11		
coarse	10	lose	4	suppose	11		
color	11	machine	12	talk	4		
cough	16	many	12	teeth	8		
country	13	March	1	terrible	18		
couple	14	marry	6	thorough	16		
course	10	material	12	though	9		
court	16	May	1	tight	4		
cousin	14	merry	6	tongue	8		
December	2	meter	22	touch	13		
die	15	most	19	tough	9		
direction	5	moth	21	towel	23		
door	18	mother	14	town	23		
double	10	move	7	trouble	10		
dough	9	north	3	type	18		
during	21	northern	3	usual	18		
dye	15	November	2	very	6		
east	3	now	23	waist	5		
eastern	3	October	2	walk	4		
else	11	odd	5	weigh	17		
enough	9	oh	10	weight	17		